Learning DevSecOps
A Practical Guide to Processes and Tools

Steve Suehring

Beijing · Boston · Farnham · Sebastopol · Tokyo

Learning DevSecOps

by Steve Suehring

Published by O'Reilly Media, Inc., 1005 Gravenstein Highway North, Sebastopol, CA 95472.

O'Reilly books may be purchased for educational, business, or sales promotional use. Online editions are also available for most titles (*http://oreilly.com*). For more information, contact our corporate/institutional sales department: 800-998-9938 or *corporate@oreilly.com*.

Acquisitions Editor: Simina Calin	**Indexer:** nSight, Inc.
Development Editor: Melissa Potter	**Interior Designer:** David Futato
Production Editors: Jonathon Owen and Clare Laylock	**Cover Designer:** Karen Montgomery
Copyeditor: nSight, Inc.	**Illustrator:** Kate Dullea
Proofreader: Piper Editorial Consulting, LLC	

May 2024:   First Edition

Revision History for the First Edition
2024-05-15:   First Release

See *http://oreilly.com/catalog/errata.csp?isbn=9781098144869* for release details.

978-1-098-14486-9

[LSI]

Table of Contents

Preface

DevSecOps jobs are abundant, but looking at the requirements for those jobs, it's quickly evident that there is no agreement on what DevSecOps actually entails. That's what made this book quite difficult to write. I've written books on everything from MySQL to JavaScript to Windows Server to Linux Firewalls. Each of those technologies has a well-defined scope. Writing on Linux firewalls does not require covering several different technologies and skills in the same book. But DevSecOps is not as well-defined. Writing on DevSecOps exposes the fissures in how we define technologies, between the actual hands-on work and the hype. Even the term "DevSecOps" is not as widely used as the term "DevOps." Granted, "DevSecOps" does not roll off the tongue as easily as "DevOps," but it's more than that. Simply lending a voice to the definition of DevSecOps is one of the reasons that I wrote this book.

The goal of this book is not to be a comprehensive step-by-step guide to implementing DevSecOps, whatever the term means. That book is impossible to write because of the rapid changes in tools and the highly customized needs of each organization moving toward DevSecOps. Rather, the goal of this book is to provide patterns of success while also exposing some of the technologies and practices involved in large DevSecOps deployments. The book does not cover every software tool that an organization might use in DevSecOps. This is not an omission, or if it is, the omission is intentional so that the focus can remain on processes and people rather than technology and tools. Tech and tooling will change, but having the best people implementing the best processes will always work.

What Is DevSecOps?

What is DevSecOps? It depends on who you ask. As defined in this book, DevSecOps is a set of agile and iterative practices that help to deliver software and technology systems rapidly, accurately, and repeatedly, emphasizing processes and people above tools.

DevSecOps is about culture first. I've worked for organizations that were so far away from agile and iterative as to be spinning backward in the software development life-cycle. In such organizations, technologies are chosen by unqualified people without any consideration for workflow, productivity, or best practices, much less the end user. Deadlines are chosen before we even know what we're building. Contrast, then, DevSecOps cultures, where testing and security are natural extensions within the development process rather than additions later on. Automation and scripting are heavily emphasized in DevOps and DevSecOps.

Computing has a great way of reinventing itself over and over again. Many of the practices shown in this book have been around since the early days of computing. Mainframes allowed for slices of computing time and resources, and that's what we do today with cloud provisioning, just on a grander scale. Many of the things we do today as modern DevSecOps practices have been around for decades on Linux. Scripting and automation is not new, but formalizing it and getting buy-in from everyone involved in an organization is the value brought by DevSecOps. That's the essence of DevSecOps: enabling people to use processes and tools to rapidly and repeatedly improve the quality of software.

Who Is This Book For?

This book is for anyone interested in learning about DevSecOps and its predecessor, DevOps. You might be involved in development, operations, or security and want to learn about the melding of all three into a set of tools and processes for making production-level deployments easier. To get maximum value from the entire book, you should have a computing background, but everyone interested in DevSecOps will benefit from Chapter 1, even those without a computing background.

Being able to write code, commit and push the code, and have tests automatically executed on that code is one such practice in DevSecOps. Scaling across multiple cloud providers is common as well. All of this is done seamlessly. Of course, all of that automation needs people who understand not only the goals of the automation but how to configure it. With that in mind, if you're interested in learning about the processes involved in DevSecOps while also being exposed to some of the technologies involved, then this book should be helpful.

How This Book Is Organized

This book is organized into eight chapters. With a few exceptions, the chapters are largely standalone, meaning that you can read only the chapters or sections of chapters that you find valuable.

Chapter 1, "The Need for DevSecOps", helps to frame the story for the rest of the book. The chapter demonstrates how software was developed with methodologies like Waterfall and Agile and how software is developed with DevSecOps. Chapter 1 also discusses the need to tear down departmental silos and places an emphasis on the importance of culture in DevSecOps.

Chapter 2, "Foundational Knowledge in 25 Pages or Less", condenses some of the most basic knowledge needed to be successful at DevSecOps—or at least lays the foundation for gaining such knowledge. If there was a way to condense weeks' worth of computing course material into one place, this is hopefully that place.

Chapter 3, "Integrating Security", continues with some of the foundational material from Chapter 2 but with a focus on security. Building on that foundation, we'll discuss the OWASP ZAP tool in Chapter 3.

Chapter 4, "Managing Code and Testing", looks at git and the Gitflow pattern in DevSecOps. The chapter also covers the various levels of testing.

Chapter 5, "Moving Toward Deployment", introduces management of configuration as code along with Docker. We'll also build a local registry for Docker.

Chapter 6, "Deploy, Operate, and Monitor", examines Ansible and Jenkins for deployment and code building. Both of these technologies are widely used, though they're certainly not the only technologies that perform deployment and build tasks. Chapter 6 also discusses monitoring, with an emphasis on best practices for monitoring.

Chapter 7, "Plan and Expand", integrates Kubernetes into the DevSecOps coverage, clustering and expanding the deployment of software in an organization.

Chapter 8, "Beyond DevSecOps", wraps up the book with coverage of five patterns and takeaways from successful DevSecOps organizations.

Conventions Used in This Book

The following typographical conventions are used in this book:

Italic
: Indicates new terms, URLs, email addresses, filenames, and file extensions.

`Constant width`
: Used for program listings, as well as within paragraphs to refer to program elements such as variable or function names, databases, data types, environment variables, statements, and keywords.

`Constant width italic`
: Shows text that should be replaced with user-supplied values or by values determined by context.

This element signifies a tip or suggestion.

 This element signifies a general note.

This element indicates a warning or caution.

O'Reilly Online Learning

O'REILLY® For more than 40 years, *O'Reilly Media* has provided technology and business training, knowledge, and insight to help companies succeed.

Our unique network of experts and innovators share their knowledge and expertise through books, articles, and our online learning platform. O'Reilly's online learning platform gives you on-demand access to live training courses, in-depth learning paths, interactive coding environments, and a vast collection of text and video from O'Reilly and 200+ other publishers. For more information, visit *https://oreilly.com*.

How to Contact Us

Please address comments and questions concerning this book to the publisher:

O'Reilly Media, Inc.
1005 Gravenstein Highway North
Sebastopol, CA 95472
800-889-8969 (in the United States or Canada)
707-827-7019 (international or local)
707-829-0104 (fax)
support@oreilly.com
https://www.oreilly.com/about/contact.html

We have a web page for this book, where we list errata, examples, and any additional information. You can access this page at *https://oreil.ly/LearningDevSecOps*.

For news and information about our books and courses, visit *https://oreilly.com*.

Find us on LinkedIn: *https://linkedin.com/company/oreilly-media*.

Watch us on YouTube: *https://youtube.com/oreillymedia*.

Acknowledgments

Thank you to the technical reviewers, Patrick Dubois, David Volm, Swapnil Shevate, and Vladislav Bilay, for their time, effort, and feedback. They helped identify areas that needed additional coverage and gave their expertise in other areas of the book. Thanks to Rob, Jim, and Jaclyn at Partners and to Tim for the assistance with review questions.

## CHAPTER 1

The Need for DevSecOps

Software is created to solve problems. However, too often, creating software comes with its own set of problems, sometimes even creating new problems along the way. An organization makes a decision whether to develop customized software or to purchase prebuilt software. The prebuilt option is most economical for commodity software like an office productivity suite. But custom development is often needed for development of advanced solutions in business functional areas. Custom solutions are created in pursuit of the ultimate goals of gaining competitive advantage or increasing efficiency.

The process of developing software changed significantly in the late 1990s and into the early 2000s. That major shift went from an intense focus on gathering requirements to a focus on iteration and speed. The iterative manner in which software is developed features repeatable processes and automation that enable rapid delivery of new features, incorporating feedback loops throughout the development lifecycle. Together with organizational cultural changes that promote an open source, transparent mentality, the result is cross-functional teams concerned more with quality than territory and merging of multiple teams: Development, Operations, and Security—DevSecOps.

This chapter looks at the drivers behind the DevSecOps movement. The process of software development is the initial focus. The evolution of software development methodologies provides the background needed to fully understand, and thus be successful at, DevSecOps. The chapter continues with an emphasis on the importance of cultural changes for organizations moving toward DevSecOps.

Developing Software

To achieve their goals, organizations allocate some of their resources to create software. It's important to consider that these resources could be invested elsewhere where the resources might gain a higher return. For example, investing $100,000 into marketing might result in more customers than investing those funds into streamlining the customer sign-up process on the website.

Even if money is not a concern, speed is. The ability to create and then deploy software quickly is a limiting factor on any effort to gain competitive advantage or increase efficiency. After a certain point, adding more developers to a project does not get that project done any faster. Just the opposite. As more developers are added, coherent communication becomes impossible.

Software starts as an idea. Taking that idea and turning it into working software requires forethought and planning. A software development project can be managed using several processes, depending in part on the type of software being developed. Software development involves defining the requirements, designing the solution, developing and coding, and finally testing the software just prior to release. This process is illustrated in Figure 1-1.

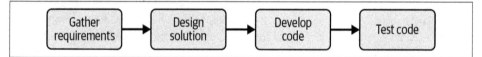

Figure 1-1. A process for software development

The four stages, sometimes called a software development lifecycle (SDLC), can be conceptualized as a waterfall, with each stage producing one or more artifacts, which are then passed or fall to the next stage, more like Figure 1-2.

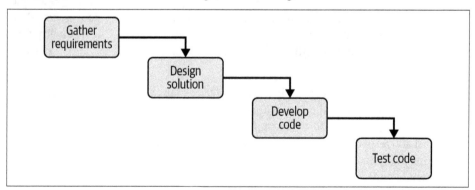

Figure 1-2. Completing each phase of a project in waterfall development

When using a methodology like waterfall to create software, each stage is completed prior to moving on to the next stage. This is illustrated within Figure 1-1 where requirements are gathered and documented before moving on to the design phase, labeled "Design solution" in Figure 1-1. If a new requirement is discovered during the design phase or additional questions lead to new requirements, those elements are frequently added into a follow-on project.

At the end of the requirements-gathering phase, the project formally has a scope defined, which includes all of the features of the software. These features incorporate the primary functions of the software along with additional features that aren't technically required for the software to function but are expected. These nonfunctional requirements are items like responsiveness or speed, security, and other behaviors of the application. Without capturing and adding the nonfunctional requirements, the resulting software product will leave users frustrated and underwhelmed.

Consider a business requirement: enabling a customer to find a product and place an order. Prior to computers, this business requirement was fulfilled in any number of ways, including the customer walking into a store, finding, and then purchasing the product or using a catalog to find the product, calling the company, and placing the order via telephone. With computers and the internet, this business requirement is now frequently accomplished through the web.

Fulfilling the business requirement of enabling a customer to find a product and place an order using a website leaves significant space to find a solution. Uploading a PDF of the catalog to the website and providing a form that enables the customer to email their order fulfills the minimal functional requirements for the site. However, even though the requirement is fulfilled, most users would expect something different and probably wouldn't order with such a clumsy process that lacks many of the features that customers take for granted within the user experience of ordering products online.

Instead, nonfunctional requirements also need to be captured. A few exploratory questions to the stakeholder or project sponsor would reveal rich detail about the intent for the solution. For example:

- How will products be represented on the site (photos, narrative, technical specifications, and so on)?
- Who will take product photos and produce them for the web, and who will write the narrative production description?
- How will inventory be updated so that customers can't order products that are out of stock?
- How will orders be placed?
- How will employees be alerted when a new order is placed?

- Who will maintain the online catalog with new products?
- What forms of payment are accepted?
- Do customers need to create accounts, track order history, track shipping?

These questions represent just a small fraction of the questions that would need to be answered during an initial exploratory or feasibility meeting. Some of these questions are already or will quickly become functional requirements during the feasibility phase or during the requirements-gathering phase. However, absent someone in the meeting who has deployed a project such as this, there would surely be missed requirements.

The scope of the project, then, defines those elements that are included and delineates other elements that are not meant to be included within a project. Anything not specifically included is assumed to be excluded and thus out of scope for the project. If a fundamental requirement was missed, the project sponsor will face the unhappy choice of redefining scope or moving forward without that requirement and then adding the missed feature in a later follow-up project.

Months or even years of calendar time can elapse between the idea and the implementation. The delay between idea and released software product makes waiting for a missed feature even more painful for the project sponsor. Within that delay, any competitive advantage that might have been realized can quickly evaporate when a competitor who didn't miss the requirement releases their own version.

The following sections examine some of the problems and associated solutions surrounding modern software development.

Developing Agility

In response to the lag between project definition and completion, organizations have turned toward iterative processes like Agile and Scrum as a means to rapidly deliver value to the stakeholder. With an iterative software development process, all four stages described earlier (requirements, design, development, and testing) are performed. Rather than attempting to capture all requirements for all possible aspects of the project, iterative development focuses on the features that are of the highest value to the stakeholder. The highest-value features are then expanded through a round of requirements gathering before being designed, developed, tested, and released, with a short cycle of two to four weeks. Figure 1-3 shows how each phase of the SDLC is handled with an iterative process like Agile.

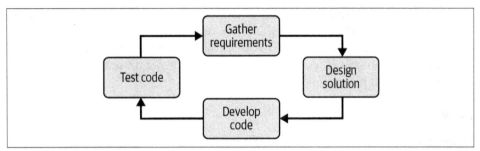

Figure 1-3. Iterating through each phase and then starting over with an Agile-like process

As illustrated in Figure 1-3, each phase is completed, but there is no attempt to gather full requirements because of the learning process associated with iterative development. If a requirement is missed, the stakeholder can choose to not release the feature or add the missed requirement in the next iteration. With an iterative development process, the next release is only weeks away rather than months or years away. Contrast that to a missed requirement in a waterfall process, where the next release may be months or years away, and you can see the clear benefit of this process.

Iterative development also enables rapid response to changing market conditions. For example, you might have the best idea for the next killer app, start development on that app, but then have your competitor release essentially the same app. In a waterfall model, you would need to scrap the project entirely. With an iterative process, focus can be shifted toward features that might be missing from the competitor's app.

Agile software development features several ceremonies such as sprint planning, daily stand-up, sprint review, sprint retrospective, and backlog grooming. An overall backlog or list of all of the possible features known at a given moment is created and prioritized. From that prioritized list of features, a sprint backlog is created. The sprint backlog is a commitment from the development team of which features will be implemented during the current iteration. The sprint backlog is created based on availability of team members and their estimation of effort, also called level of effort (LOE), for each individual item on the backlog.

At the end of the sprint, a sprint review is conducted where the team shows off what it has accomplished during that iteration. After the sprint review has been completed, the team examines what might have been done differently during the sprint within the retrospective. A team might answer three questions during the retrospective:

- What should we start doing?
- What should we stop doing?
- What should we continue doing?

These three questions enable the team to reflect on what worked, what didn't work, and what they might change moving into the next iteration. With the retrospective complete, the team can move toward backlog grooming, where the product backlog is refined and reprioritized. The stakeholder or product owner is usually involved in the backlog refinement process to set priority for the team.

Developing Broken Software

Flawed requirements lead to flawed software, or software that doesn't meet the original requirement. Flawed software can happen regardless of whether that original requirement was successfully elicited from the project sponsor. The end result is dissatisfaction, broken functionality, and security problems.

When examining the requirements, developers are often left with questions. These questions range from the mundane, such as where to place the curly braces for a conditional in some languages, to the critical, such as obtaining credentials for a database connection. In the latter case, development may need to stop while those credentials are obtained. In other cases, developers simply answer the question to the best of their ability and keep moving forward.

Developing software in a silo, devoid of interaction with anyone other than developers, leads to broken software. In the siloed development style, using a waterfall or similar methodology, the developers examine and interpret requirements to the best of their ability. Consider the following question: "In which web browsers should the site work?" along with a common answer: "Browsers? I've been developing using Chrome; I didn't think about the site working in other browsers." Figure 1-4 illustrates development in a silo, where developers, operations staff, and security engineers don't communicate well.

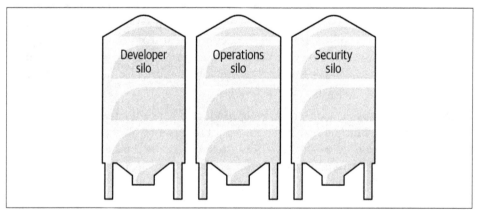

Figure 1-4. Siloed development in an organization leads to lack of visibility

Deadlines dictate the number of features and the quality of those features. The deadline for delivery may be such that there is no time to even identify the issues that might occur when testing using a different browser or different viewport such as a phone, much less fix those issues. If cross-browser testing was not included as a step in the project and the browsers in which the site must work were not specified in the requirements, then it's anyone's guess as to which browsers the site will work in.

Deadlines, or the timeline of the project, is one of the three levers that can be controlled within a software development project. The other two levers are cost and features. The adage is that a given project can choose two of the three, meaning that if the project needs to be done quickly and with many features, then costs will increase. Likewise, if a project needs many features but low costs, then completing the project will take longer. Finally, if costs must be kept as low as possible while still meeting the deadline, then features are the first thing to be sacrificed.

Figure 1-5 illustrates the concept of the software development triangle.

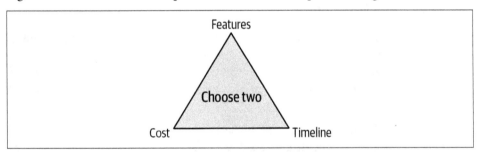

Figure 1-5. Choose two of the three elements at any one time

The next problem I'll address is the handoff between development and QA.

Operating in a Darkroom

Somewhere between development and testing lies an all-too-often awkward handoff between those who developed the software and those who are now charged with deploying, operating, and supporting the software in its production environment: the operations team. The operations team may be known by many names, including network administrators, system administrators, or engineering (site reliability engineer [SRE], production engineers, and the like), among others.

The operations team needs to take software that may never have been tested on a computing environment like the one in production and run it according to the service-level agreement (SLA) needed by the organization. That software may have only been tested on developer workstations and then a small quality assurance (QA) environment. The QA environment may have an entirely different configuration—for example, it may be lacking a load balancer, may be deployed in a different region, and may be significantly less busy than its production counterpart. Nevertheless, the software is deployed into production, and the operations team needs to support it.

Consider this scenario: up until the moment that the software was deployed, everything worked well. There was virtually no latency for any requests, and even when all of the developers were working on the site, response times were unremarkable. Unnoticed was that the developers were using a server that was physically located on the same local area network (LAN) as they were and that the data being used by the application came from a nonproduction replica that rarely receives any requests.

When the software was deployed to production by the operations team, the site was instantly underperforming to the point of being unusable. Users logging in were unable to continue because sessions were spread across multiple servers instead of just the one that the developers were using during the entire development lifecycle. And then you have the security problem.

Security as an Afterthought

A "ship at any cost" mentality can exist in some organizations along with a "minimally viable product" (MVP) attitude. While in theory such a development paradigm might work, the assumption is that there will be time allocated to circle around and fix the issues that made the software "minimally viable" in the first place. That time rarely exists.

When deadlines loom, security seems to be the first requirement to be sacrificed, assuming security was thought of at all. Much like math, security is hard. Security analysts need to be right every time, while an attacker only needs to be right once.

Too often, the data security department within an organization is seen as the department that says "no." Whether you're talking about a request for a new application, a firewall change, or relaxing rules on database access, the people tasked with maintaining security necessarily lean toward saying no when a change request comes through.

The inherent problem both with operations and data security is that they are invisible until something goes wrong. In the case of data security, much time is spent responding to compliance audits that seemingly add very little value to day-to-day security for many organizations. Make no mistake, legal and regulatory compliance is essential, but regulations often lag reality, meaning that the regulations capture compliance against yesterday's vulnerability while the attackers are using the latest zero-day.

In the context of DevSecOps, security integration is necessary early so that firewall changes or noncompliant methods of accessing and storing data are never even considered. Without security integration, a developer might use unencrypted passwords or store credentials in the source code management system, potentially exposing them to individuals who are not authorized to view the data.

This section addressed many of the issues associated with software development, some of which are solved with DevOps and DevSecOps. Next, I'll dive into how your organization's culture can determine your success with DevSecOps.

Culture First

Organizational culture is the primary factor that determines whether DevSecOps will be successful. A control-oriented, top-down organization will struggle with the changes necessary to truly implement DevSecOps. Such an organization may use technology that feels like DevSecOps, but the cultural shift toward cross-team pollination will prevent true success.

A certain appreciation for the importance of cultural fit is not possible unless and until you've experienced trying to implement Agile-like practices in a rigid control-oriented organization. In such an organization, the best solution is less important than subordination and maintaining separation to keep control at the top. Without that experience, it might be possible to believe that culture plays no role in DevSecOps success.

Of course, anarchy and chaos isn't the goal of DevSecOps. Instead, DevSecOps facilitates a problem-solving approach even if the solution comes from someone in a different department. Some may believe that DevSecOps thrives when used with a startup mentality (historically a much more flexible culture), but the movement is much more nuanced than that.

A startup mentality implies both competitiveness and innovation, breaking new ground without regard to hierarchy. The founder of a startup frequently works alongside employees as their peer, possibly mentor, to drive the product forward. In a startup, job titles are less important than ensuring that the work is accomplished.

Within DevSecOps, people work together across job functions, using their skills where needed. Like a startup, the team is transparent about their work, focusing on the end goal of accomplishing useful work. In such an environment, potential problems can be identified and addressed early, well before that problem becomes visible.

> ## DevOps Without Sec
>
> Before DevSecOps, there was DevOps (Development and Operations). However, the realization soon occurred that development and operations cannot be successful without meaningful integration of security best practices. By integrating security discussions at project inception, security can become pervasive but not invasive.
>
> DevOps can exist and be helpful even if the organization is not ready to fully integrate security. However, the same problems that led to the DevOps movement, where problems with a deployment are not found until too late, can happen because of the (necessary) security controls in place within the production or live environment. When that occurs, momentum builds toward DevSecOps as a cultural change.

The next section looks at the core of DevOps, which is an emphasis on processes versus the tools used to implement those processes.

Processes over Tools

DevOps and DevSecOps are more about processes than the tools used to implement those processes. Without the cultural fit and changes to process, the tooling used in DevSecOps often gets in the way of progress and sometimes slows development down. Even if an organization isn't ready to make the cultural changes needed for true DevSecOps, some benefit is possible by using a few of the best practices underlying DevSecOps. Let's explore a few of those now, starting with knowing how to recognize the talent who will embrace DevSecOps.

Promoting the Right Skills

Management buy-in and visible commitment to DevSecOps processes is the absolute final arbiter over whether DevSecOps will be successful. Merely having teams talk to one another is a first step, though likely more symbolic than productive. Managers can't expect to bring people together who have interests that sometimes clash and expect magic to happen.

The processes involved in finding value with DevSecOps require varied skill sets that cut across functional areas. For example, a developer that also deploys their own clusters and can articulate the difference between DNS and DHCP is a candidate for a DevSecOps pilot program within an organization. Therefore, identifying the employees who have cross-functional experience is the true first step. Those individuals can be used to champion efforts around DevSecOps.

Identifying eclectic skills and then enabling employees with those skills to cross functional boundaries is the first step of the process and illustrates the importance of management and executive buy-in for DevSecOps. Developers will need access to, or at least visibility into, server and network areas that may have been solely under the purview of Operations. Operations and Security staff will need to have substantive early input within the project lifecycle so that they can provide feedback to improve downstream processes. For example, a change for a project in development will increase disk utilization immensely. However, with a slight change to the project, utilization can be shifted onto a different system. The opportunity to implement that change would only be available early in the development process, which is why having Operations staff substantively involved in every project is important.

DevSecOps as Process

The process of DevSecOps brings people from different functional areas together. Once together, the goal is to produce better software—software that meets requirements and is delivered rapidly and accurately. The process of delivering this software can, and frequently does, involve tooling. Let's explore some of the processes in this next section.

Hammers and screwdrivers

Tools are essential to complete some jobs efficiently. A roofer used a nail gun attached to a compressed air tank to attach shingles to my roof. That same job could have been done using a hammer but would have been much more difficult to accomplish with a screwdriver. Sure, the contractor could've used the handle of the screwdriver to drive the nails through, but doing so would have been slow and inefficient and would have resulted in nails being bent and shingles being damaged. Put me on the roof trying to handle the nail gun, and there would have been at least one trip to the emergency room.

DevSecOps is similar. Just as properly roofing a building takes a combination of skilled workers and tools, DevSecOps requires tools and the know-how to use the tools properly. Just as a powerful nail gun is the right tool when used by a qualified person, DevSecOps tooling can provide huge efficiency gains when used by the right people.

The tool should help complete the job, but the tool does not define the job.

Repeatability

DevSecOps focuses on building repeatable processes, which then facilitates automation. Or perhaps it is the other way around. Automation facilitates repeatable processes. Yes, both are true. Automating the creation of environments and the deployment of code enables those processes to be repeated, time and again, with the same result. Automated testing relieves the burden of needing to manually test and retest the same areas of code, even after changes or bug fixes have been implemented.

When implementing processes and tools to assist in repeatability, an "as Code" paradigm comes to the foreground in organizations practicing DevSecOps. "Infrastructure as Code," "Configuration as Code," "Everything as Code" are terms that all refer to the same concept: manage as much as possible using source code management tools and processes.

Most servers use text files or text-like files to store configuration elements. These text files can be stored in a source code management tool such as Git. Doing so enables versioning of configuration changes. For example, other administrators can look back through the commit history and see that I used an underscore in a DNS hostname once and took thousands of domains offline. At least that repository is not publicly available, so no one will find my mistake. In seriousness, versioning configuration changes makes for rapid recovery if there is an issue caused by a configuration change. Source code management practices for server configurations also facilitate versioning, meaning that developers can deploy a certain set of configurations to re-create a bug being reported using the same environment.

The same set of configurations with the same versions of software makes software deployment repeatable. Repeatable deployment is directly connected to continuous integration/continuous deployment (CI/CD) scenarios, where code is automatically tested and promoted through a series of environments before being promoted to the production environment. An administrator changes a configuration element for a service, commits the configuration file, and pushes the change to the remote repository where the change is noticed and deployment is automatically started to the appropriate servers.

I'm purposefully ignoring the numerous formats that are used to store configurations such as Yet Another Markup Language (YAML), INI file structure, Extensible Markup Language (XML), JavaScript Object Notation, brew scripts, m4 commands, and any other structure that can be edited with a text editor like Vim. For the purposes of this book, and unless doing so would cause undue confusion, you'll see all of these formats simply referred to as text files. Here's an example of YAML:

```
- name: add docker apt key
    apt_key:
      url: https://download.docker.com/linux/debian/gpg
      state: present

- name: add docker repo
    apt_repository:
      repo: deb [arch=amd64] \
https://download.docker.com/linux/debian stretch stable
      state: present
```

Visibility

DevSecOps also serves to enable visibility throughout the development process. Not only is there frequent visibility through an Agile ceremony like Daily Standup, but there's also visibility through the tooling that deploys code automatically to environments on demand. Members of a DevSecOps team can see exactly which code and configurations exist in which environments and can deploy new environments as needed.

Reliability, speed, and scale

Repeatability and visibility lead to reliability. Code and environments can be deployed consistently, time and again, in the same way. If there is an error during deployment, that error is found immediately because of the visibility inherent in the deployment tools and processes. With reliability then comes speed, or the ability to quickly react to changing needs. That change may be a need to scale up or down based on demand, which is possible and no longer difficult because of the repeatable and reliable processes involved in deployment.

Microservices and architectural features

Though not directly required for DevSecOps, the use of microservices can serve as an enabler of speed and scale. With microservices, small functional areas of code are identified and separated such that those functional areas can stand on their own, providing a consistent application programming interface (API) to other services within the architecture. The API is frequently expressed through an HTTP web service. Being standalone, microservices can be developed and deployed separately from other services or functional areas, thereby further increasing overall speed and development momentum.

This section looked at some of the processes involved in DevOps and DevSecOps. The next section expands on the SDLC shown earlier in the chapter, incorporating the ideas behind the processes to create an expanded SDLC for DevSecOps.

The DevSecOps SDLC

By this point, hopefully you have a feel for some of the problems inherent in software development; even relatively new methods of development like Agile foster a silo mentality. Instead of the four-phase model shown in Figure 1-2, an eight-phase model has been created. This model incorporates planning, development, and testing along with other tasks and is shown in Figure 1-6.

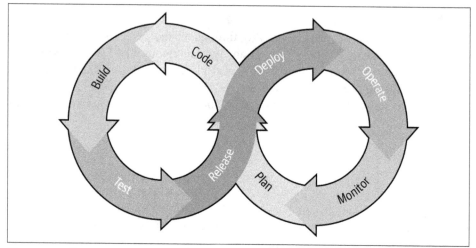

Figure 1-6. Creating a new SDLC for DevOps

The primary advantage to the DevOps SDLC is that it more closely reflects what actually happens for software development. Much more time is spent coding and testing the software than planning to code and test the software, but the interim "build" step reflects the assembly stage where the various pieces that comprise a modern application are connected to one another. Likewise, the "release" step reflects the need for multiple components along with potential approval gates through which the software must pass to begin deployment. Not captured in the SDLCs covered in this chapter is the need to both operate and monitor the software after it goes live. Without the "operate" and "monitor" phases, the Operations team becomes invisible again.

You may have noticed that "Sec" has been temporarily dropped in the last paragraph and in Figure 1-6. That's because DevOps was its own movement prior to adding security in the middle. It's clear that there is a need for security, but where should it go? Conceptually and practically, it would be difficult to implement security as its own phase. If "add security" is a new phase and is done after planning, then what happens when a security issue is introduced during coding? Adding the security phase after or during testing or to the release phase is also difficult. What happens if a serious security issue arises? Does the entire project grind to a halt to remediate the problem? Relegating security even later, to operations and monitoring, effectively means that the issue will occur in the production environment, with the inherent danger brought by a live production security problem.

Instead, security is usually shown as underlying each phase. You may see security illustrated as in Figure 1-7.

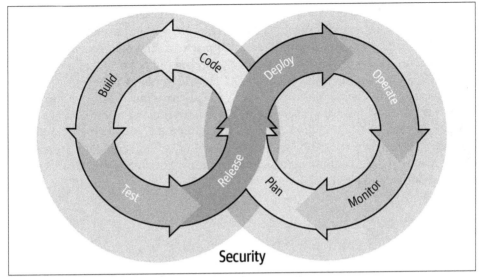

Figure 1-7. Security is part of every phase of a DevSecOps SDLC

Security is usually depicted in this way to highlight the need to incorporate security and security-oriented processes at every phase of software development. This alleviates the need to determine where a security phase should appear or what to do when a security issue is found.

The expansion of the SDLC from the four-phase model to the newer eight-phase model, wrapped by security, enables practitioners of DevSecOps to reflect the processes that encompass modern software development. Importantly, the tasks completed in each phase were happening behind the scenes anyway. The DevSecOps SDLC merely highlights those tasks. These phases will be examined throughout the remainder of the book.

Summary

DevSecOps comes as a natural progression of software development. From Agile processes and a transparent open source mentality, DevSecOps works to break down silos that slow down development and make development less reliable. Cultural changes, started at the top of an organization, are the primary key element to achieving the most benefit from DevSecOps. Barring the commitment from management, DevSecOps can devolve into more tooling that is only half-used. However, with cultural changes and a breakdown of barriers between teams, tools can be added to facilitate the repeatability, visibility, reliability, speed, and scaling needed by modern organizations.

From here, the book examines common DevSecOps practices using the content from Figure 1-7 as a guide. Each chapter covers one or more of the phases in the DevSecOps SDLC. There is a specific focus on processes and practices and coverage of select tools used within those phases. Prior to beginning on the infinite path of DevSecOps, Chapter 2 contains foundational knowledge that will be helpful for the later chapters of the book. Many readers will already have much, if not more, of this knowledge already. Likewise, many readers will have notions of some of the areas covered in Chapter 2, depending on their background. Of course, the technologies covered in Chapter 2 may also be entirely new. But as the book goes deeper into DevSecOps, having a common and shared definition for often-overloaded technical terms will be helpful for all.

CHAPTER 2

Foundational Knowledge in 25 Pages or Less

During the latter part of my career, I have taught on the beautiful campus of University of Wisconsin–Stevens Point. The computing program at UWSP enables students to pursue degrees in multiple subjects and emphases. The classroom experience demonstrated the need for students to gain exposure to topics outside of their major or emphasis. For example, students within a development-focused major found value from experience with command-line tools and traditionally operations-focused areas like DNS. Likewise, students within networking and server tracks were helped by learning programmatic techniques for scripting.

If there is a common technological skill that all DevSecOps practitioners need to be familiar with, it's working in a shell or terminal, also known as a command-line environment. Whether creating scripts and configuration files, running commands, or troubleshooting errors in logfiles, the command line is central to becoming adept at DevSecOps and even in your specific role as a developer, security admin, or operator. Command-line skills are a differentiator toward going to the next level with DevSecOps.

This chapter provides a high-level overview of many of the subjects that many organizations encounter while working toward and with DevSecOps practices and processes. If I polled 100 people with some computing experience, there would be at least 101 different responses for subject matter coverage. With that in mind, the chapter will not attempt to cover the breadth of subjects that you might need at some point during your career or your DevSecOps journey. The chapter will also not be able to provide the depth of coverage needed on each subject. Entire degree programs are designed to provide that depth.

The chapter begins with an introduction to the command-line interface before continuing with coverage of the basic networking models in use today. DNS is included in the chapter due to its importance for troubleshooting and for some knowledge sharing that will be helpful as discussions between teams occur in DevSecOps.

The Command-Line Interface

If there was a single differentiator between computing professionals, those who hold a job role related to computing, and hardcore hobbyists, that differentiator would be the use of the command-line interface (CLI). Many network and computing devices have CLIs through which the devices can be managed quickly and efficiently. The vast majority of the busiest sites on the internet and backbone services of the internet are BSD- or Linux-based, and desktop graphical user interfaces (GUIs) are not used or even installed. This makes the CLI an essential part of the job. Automation, configuration, and scripting are all centered around the CLI in most modern environments.

Command Line Versus Terminal Versus Shell

What I've been referring to as the command-line interface goes by many names. You may hear command line, command-line interface, command prompt, command-line environment, shell, shell prompt, shell environment, terminal, SSH, or some variation thereof. While there are some key differences, the large majority of these differences are unimportant to the DevSecOps practitioner.

The shell is a program that provides a CLI into a computing device. Just as there are many programs that seem to do the same thing, so too are there many shell programs. A common shell is known as Bourne-again shell or bash. It is common enough and widely available, and thus I will assume bash unless specified otherwise for the remainder of the book. If you're using a Mac or Linux, then you have a shell installed, available through Terminal. It's worth noting that depending on the version of macOS, the default shell could be bash or Z shell.

 Capitalization is an issue when writing about bash. When the word "bash" appears at the beginning of a sentence, you need to capitalize it. However, when referring to bash as a command, it should be lowercase because it will be lowercase on whatever system you're using the command or shell on. Here's my advice: ignore any differences in capitalization that you see when referring to bash. I promise not to use that as a license to capitalize "bash" in new ways, but you may see "Bash" on occasion, both in this book and on the internet. "Bash" and "bash" are the same in this format, but the command itself will always be lowercase when using it. Luckily, you will typically only use the word "Bash" as the opening line to scripts that you write.

Not All CLIs Are Created Equal

The command prompt in Windows provides an interface based on DOS (Disk Operating System) and has severely limited capability when compared with a more robust shell environment of the type found on Linux. PowerShell for Windows is an improvement over the command prompt and enables full scripted access to the Windows environment. However, in recognition of the importance of Linux, Microsoft created the Windows Subsystem for Linux (WSL), which provides a nearly full Linux experience and enables Windows users to utilize a CLI by installing one or more popular Linux distributions.

The process for installing WSL has evolved over the last several years, and WSL itself is now known as WSL 2. I haven't yet found a consistent "this always works" means to install WSL on a Windows build due to the many different configurations and features that may be installed on a given Windows system. Even a Windows installer that I received from Bill Gates didn't work to install WSL 2 on the first try and without a series of reboots. With that out of the way, you'll find the instructions for installing WSL 2 in the WSL documentation (*https://learn.microsoft.com/en-us/windows/wsl/install*).

Why Do I Need the Command Line?

I've heard variations of the question "Why do I need the command line [or SSH or Terminal]?" for many years. The answer is simple: speed. Much (possibly all) of the work of a DevSecOps practitioner can be done faster and more efficiently from a CLI. When using a CLI, your hands never need to leave the keyboard in order to click a menu or button.

When programming, an editor like Vim can be used entirely from the home position on the keyboard, and the software involved in security and operations will have a command to run, whether in addition to a GUI or whether as its sole means to execute the program.

A very simple use case for the CLI, including a WSL Linux install, is to create a backup of important files. The rsync command can be used to synchronize or transfer files from your local machine to a shared storage or a backup USB drive. I maintain a music library for DJs that is somewhere under 20,000 files across a deep hierarchy of directories. The files are stored in both a large/uncompressed version and then in several other formats that have smaller file sizes. The rsync command is used to create backups of these files. If something happens to the network connection or the process stops for some reason, rsync will pick up from where it left off. When files are added, rsync will only send the changed files rather than all of the files again.

Getting Started with the Command Line

If you're using Mac or Linux, you already have a full-featured CLI at your disposal through a Terminal window. If you're on a Mac, then the Terminal, found under Applications → Utilities, will place you directly into a CLI. Accessing the CLI on Linux varies depending on distribution and means of access. If there's a desktop environment, then you will typically find a terminal program. Otherwise, using Secure Shell (SSH) to connect to the Linux computer will also work.

If you're on a Microsoft Windows 10 or 11 computer, then installing WSL 2 (*https://learn.microsoft.com/en-us/windows/wsl/install*) is an easy way to get started. If you're on an earlier version of Windows or cannot install WSL 2, then virtualization software like VirtualBox (*https://www.virtualbox.org*) will enable you to install a full copy of a Linux distribution.

Later in this chapter and throughout the book, the command line will be used frequently. In addition, Appendix B contains a select group of commands to help navigate in the command line. Now let's move from the command line into a high-level overview of protocols.

Protocols: A High-Level Overview

The internet communicates through a series of protocols. When thinking of communication, protocol is merely an agreement on how each party will act. Consider a voice conversation on a telephone. One party places the call, which causes the receiving party to answer with some form of "Hello" or similar statement. The party who placed the call then responds with a greeting, maybe also "Hello." The calling party may follow their greeting with an introduction and may also state the purpose of the call.

That narrative describes the typical protocol for a voice call, where each side is expected to act in a certain way. Consider what happens when the protocol breaks for whatever reason. Sometimes an incoming call may arrive just as the receiver is picking up the handset, in which case they may not know that there was an incoming call and therefore won't say "Hello" to initiate the conversation. More common with robocallers is for the receiver to answer "Hello," which is then followed by a long pause while the robocalling software connects to a real person on their side. This introduces the concept of a timeout to protocols. When the receiver answers with "Hello," they typically expect a response within a short timeframe. If not, then there's a strong indication that the call is a robocall.

The discussion of protocols around telephone conversations can be extended to many human interactions on a daily basis. Without protocols, there would be chaos. Computers, especially network communications, are built around conformance to protocols. Just as with human interaction, those protocols ensure interoperability.

Without protocols, each vendor would have their own implementation of every form of communication, and rarely would those communication methods be compatible. Want to send an email to someone who uses products from a different vendor? You'd need to sign up for that network and use proprietary software to do so.

Instead of the nightmare of noninteroperable software, the internet is built on common, shared, and open protocols—mostly. The basis of communication is Internet Protocol (IP), which has various means to be transported from point to point, from device to device. Many other common and foundational network services are similar and rely on IP as the basis of communication. This section examines protocol layers and related models for networking.

Protocol Layers

Communication related to networks is typically represented by one of two models, the Open Systems Interconnect (OSI) model (*https://en.wikipedia.org/wiki/OSI_model*) or the TCP/IP model (*https://en.wikipedia.org/wiki/Internet_protocol_suite*). The OSI model is depicted in Figure 2-1.

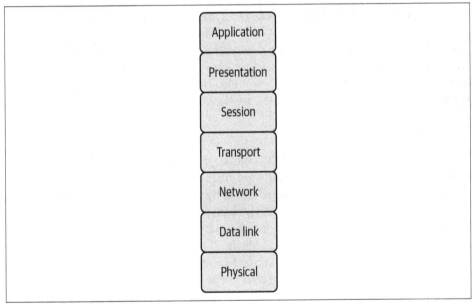

Figure 2-1. The layers of the OSI model

The TCP/IP model is similar, except that the session, presentation, and application layers are converted into a single application layer, and the data link and physical layers are combined into a single local Link or local network layer. This is depicted in Figure 2-2.

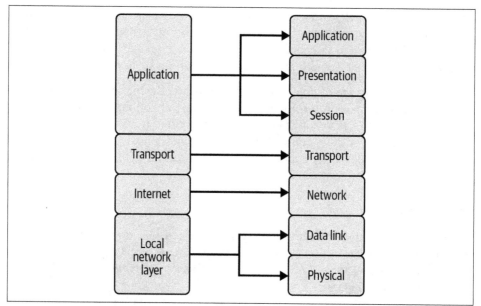

Figure 2-2. Comparing the TCP/IP model (left) to the OSI model (right)

When devices communicate over a network, the data is passed down the layers from an application such as a web browser and eventually onto a physical medium such as wired Ethernet or radio signals for WiFi. The receiver then passes the data up through the layers to the corresponding application on the receiving side.

Two Protocols Plus Another

Transmission Control Protocol (TCP) and User Datagram Protocol (UDP) are the most common protocols that you will encounter on a daily basis. TCP is connection-oriented, and UDP is connectionless. This difference means that applications using TCP should receive packets in an orderly sequence, whereas applications using UDP are responsible for ensuring that packets have arrived and for asking for retransmission when packets have not arrived. Much of what will matter to the DevSecOps practitioner relies on TCP, with a notable exception around the Domain Name System (DNS) protocol, which is covered later in this chapter.

An outlier protocol that doesn't quite fit is Internet Control Message Protocol (ICMP) (*https://www.iana.org/assignments/icmp-parameters/icmp-parameters.xhtml*). ICMP is the protocol behind the ping command that you might use to verify connectivity. This chapter will not deep-dive into ICMP beyond the superficial. However, within the context of ICMP, there are various message types that are used by routers and network devices to note network states. When using the ping command, you are sending ICMP message type 8, "Echo Request," and, if the device under test responds, it will respond with "Echo Reply," also known as ICMP message type 0.

Why Does This Matter?

If you're a developer looking to learn about DevSecOps, you may have already asked, "Why does any of this matter?" or "How will it help me?" These are valid questions to ask. Learning protocols and protocol layers matters because DevSecOps is the most successful when each team understands more about the other teams. Security analysts and operations staff must be familiar with protocols, if for nothing else than to be able to open ports in the firewall. Developers can get those ports open faster by expressing the need in a way that makes sense to security analysts, such as, "This application requires tcp/443 outbound" rather than "It needs to connect to their server to activate."

Basic Internet Protocols

The previous section provided a brief definition of a protocol followed by a closer inspection of two models that represent the layered nature of communication for the internet. This section continues the exploration of protocols by covering some of the basic internet-related protocols that will be encountered regularly by those working in DevSecOps organizations. The section begins with DNS, which provides the foundation on which other services rely. It is notable that this section and indeed this book intentionally skip coverage of protocol headers. Though there will be coverage of IP addressing, and I cover simplistic differences between TCP and UDP, being able to recite the TCP three-way handshake is not necessary.

Throughout this section and the remainder of the book, you will see the term "RFC" or its plural, "RFCs." RFCs, or Requests for Comments, are the standards by which the internet operates. Created by the Internet Engineering Task Force (IETF), RFCs are responsible for codifying the expected behavior of software and hardware. More information on RFCs and the process behind them can be found on the IETF website (*https://ietf.org/standards/rfcs*).

DNS

The Domain Name System (DNS) is the reason that we do not need to remember IP addresses to communicate and obtain information on the internet. Technically, name resolution itself does that, and there are other means for providing name resolution. But maintaining a text file containing every possible host that I might want to communicate with would be cumbersome. Therefore, DNS is the focal point for name resolution on the internet.

DNS is defined by RFCs 1034 and 1035 and provides a hierarchical method for sharing responsibility for domains of control and the naming of nodes or hosts. At the root of the DNS is a single dot that branches out to several top-level domains (TLDs). TLDs are general, such as *com*, *net*, *edu*, and numerous others. TLDs can also be country code top-level domains (ccTLDs), such as *uk* or *de*. Figure 2-3 shows the hierarchical nature of the DNS.

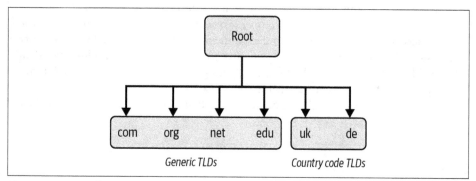

Figure 2-3. DNS hierarchy

Prior to the opening of TLDs to the public, there were just a handful of general TLDs. Now there are many generic TLDs. The Root Zone Database (*https://www.iana.org/domains/root/db*) contains a list of current TLDs.

Domains are registered by individuals and organizations within the desired TLD and according to the rules of the registrar who has been delegated the authority for that TLD. A typical registration of a domain in the com TLD lasts for a year and has a small cost associated with it. Registration of a domain requires at least two authoritative name servers, with the term "authoritative" having special meaning in this context.

When a domain is registered, control of the naming within that domain is delegated to the registrant, the person or organization who has registered the domain. The DNS servers associated with that domain are authoritative, meaning that when a query is sent about a host in that domain, the query is sent to one of the authoritative servers, which then responds accordingly.

Hostname resolution

Assuming that the host has a valid IP address and one or more DNS servers available, when that host would like to begin communicating on a network, the host needs to translate the friendly name to an IP address to determine where to send the message. Most computers and servers will first examine a file stored locally called "*hosts.*" The *hosts* file is stored in */etc/* on macOS and Linux systems and is found in the *%SystemRoot%\System32\Drivers\etc* directory on newer versions of Windows. The contents of the *hosts* file vary but generally contain information about the localhost address. For example, the file */etc/hosts* on macOS Big Sur contains the following:

```
##
# Host Database
#
# localhost is used to configure the loopback interface
# when the system is booting.  Do not change this entry.
##
127.0.0.1       localhost
255.255.255.255 broadcasthost
::1             localhost
```

Both Android and iOS systems also contain *hosts* files, but editing those files is more difficult and not typically something done by a DevSecOps engineer.

Because the *hosts* file is queried first, there is an opportunity to hijack or bypass the normal name resolution process. Doing so can be helpful for development and testing when the developer would like requests to be sent to their local computer or a computer different than the one defined in DNS. However, assuming that the destination computer is not defined within the *hosts* file, the DNS is queried next.

In broad terms, each device that receives an IP address typically also receives one or more DNS servers that act on behalf of those devices to obtain hostnames from other DNS servers. The words "typically" and "receives" both have special meaning. There is no requirement that DNS servers are included or used. A host can receive an IP address without a DNS server and communicate without issue, assuming that the host either has a local *hosts* file or does not use hostnames for communication. In addition, the word "receives" can mean anything from manually assigning IP information or obtaining it through an automated means such as Dynamic Host Configuration Protocol (DHCP).

These DNS servers are known as resolvers because they provide hostname resolution. If you're reading this on a device connected to a WiFi network, then you may have a DNS server on your local network that is responsible for obtaining the IP address when you attempt to go to *google.com*.

Note the difference between a resolver and an authoritative name server. A resolver is responsible for obtaining answers to queries from client devices, even if that resolver is not responsible or authoritative for the domain in question. An authoritative name server is the owner or authority for one or more domains. It's possible for a resolver to be authoritative for one or more domains too, but logically, hostname resolution and authoritative name resolution are two different things. Technically, "recursive resolution" or "recursive resolver" is the term you might hear for a DNS resolver that goes and gets the answer for you, but for the purposes of this chapter, knowing that there is a difference between a resolver and an authoritative nameserver is sufficient.

Figure 2-4 shows a DNS resolution from a client computer to its local resolver, which then queries the authoritative *google.com* server for the IP address of *google.com*. The reply is returned to the resolver, which then passes the answer back to the client.

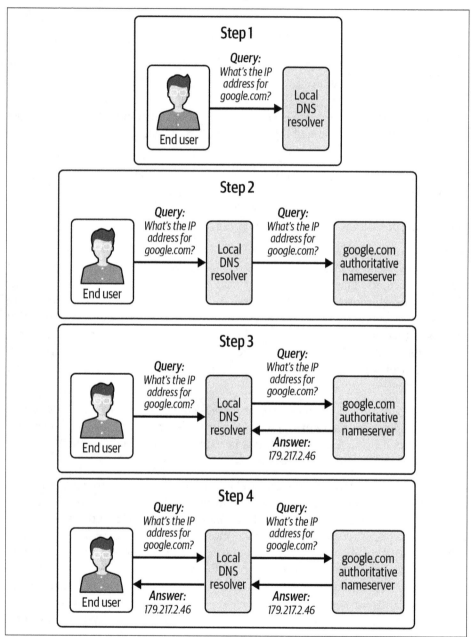

Figure 2-4. DNS resolution

Figure 2-5 demonstrates what happens when the local resolver is also authoritative for a domain. While this situation is rare for a home user, it is much more common for an enterprise scenario and thus more important to understand for the DevSecOps engineer.

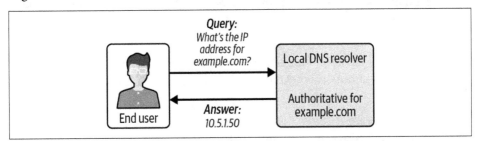

Figure 2-5. Receiving an answer from a local authoritative DNS server

Additionally, in an enterprise scenario, there may be a split authority that results in a hostname resolving to an internal IP address when queried from internally but resolving to a different IP address when queried externally. There are several reasons for this scenario, including ease of testing and the ability to control traffic flows. Figure 2-6 illustrates this scenario; note the different answers for the same query depending on who is asking.

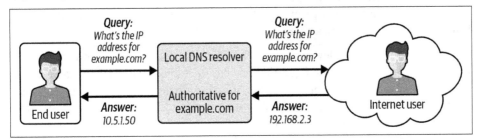

Figure 2-6. Split DNS

The figures should help to illustrate the complexity involved in DNS and why DNS can be responsible for difficulty when moving from development to testing to production.

Start of Authority and time-to-live

Before this turns into a book on DNS, of which there are many—including an authoritative work called *DNS and BIND* by Cricket Liu and Paul Albitz (O'Reilly, 2006)—there is one more thing to briefly cover. Each DNS zone contains a Start of Authority (SOA) record that defines domain metadata. Some of the highlights relevant to the DevSecOps practitioner include:

Serial number

An integer value that is incremented for each change to the zone

Refresh

The amount of time in seconds that a secondary DNS server waits before asking for updates

Retry

The amount of time in seconds that a secondary server should wait between requests to an unresponsive server

Expire

The amount of time in seconds that a primary server can be down before it is no longer considered authoritative for the domain

NX

The amount of time in seconds that a negative or not-found answer should be cached before a recursive server checks again

In addition to the values stored in the SOA itself, there is a time-to-live (TTL) value that is configured for the entire domain and can also be configured on a per-record basis. The TTL controls how long a recursive server will cache the information about a given record before asking again. The longer the TTL, the less load there is on the authoritative nameserver. However, the longer the TTL, the longer the amount of time that may elapse before a change is noticed by recursive servers.

From the standpoint of DevSecOps, DNS TTLs come to the foreground when there is either downtime or a configuration change that requires DNS changes. When you know of a pending deployment that requires changes to DNS records, a best practice is to lower the TTL for the affected records such that it will take less time for the change to propagate. The trade-off between higher load on the DNS server is typically offset by shorter downtime associated with a smaller TTL.

By lowering the TTL you are forcing resolvers everywhere to ask for the new IP address information. Lowering the TTL requires planning because the existing TTL value needs to expire before the new one goes into effect. For example, if the TTL for an A record is 604,800 seconds, or 7 days, then it won't matter much if you change the TTL the night before the deployment because any resolvers that asked for name resolution have another 6 days before they might ask again. Therefore, knowing the existing TTL and planning for deployments that require DNS changes is required.

Appendix B contains some helpful commands to use when troubleshooting DNS. Included within the appendix, you'll find the dig command for determining the TTL for a given DNS record, along with basic Linux commands, among other things.

HTTP

Hypertext Transfer Protocol (HTTP) is a core protocol for the DevSecOps practitioner. HTTP is the language of the web and is used for transferring web pages and remote programmatic access between services. HTTP is defined by several RFCs but primarily RFC 9110 along with RFC 9112; for the purposes of this section, I will ignore encryption-related matters because those are largely irrelevant at the protocol-specific level.

HTTP is a stateless protocol, meaning that the client, such as your computer, makes a request to a web server, a server that speaks HTTP. The server does not remember one request to the next; each request is new. When a client makes a request, that request follows the protocol defined in the RFCs. HTTP exchanges, or messages, consist of control data, headers, content, and trailers. In practice, you will most likely encounter control data, headers, and content when working with HTTP, and you will most likely hear of control data as part of the HTTP headers, which provides an important distinction.

Protocol elements that belong in the header section may not be allowed in the content. Therefore, when the header section is closed within a response, no additional headers can be sent. This can sometimes be a point of confusion for developers working with sessions, cookies, and other elements to build a more complex web application.

The beginning of an HTTP exchange starts with the client sending a request to the server for a certain resource such as a web page. That request will include a method or a verb in addition to several other pieces of metadata for the request itself. A commonly used HTTP method is GET, where the client is asking to retrieve, or "get," a resource from the server. If the server has that resource, then it will respond to the client with a message followed by the page or resource being requested. Here's an example:

```
GET /devops.php HTTP/1.1
Host: www.example.com
```

In this basic example, an HTTP method of GET is used to request a file called *devops.php* located at / or the document root. The version of HTTP being used for the request is included and is 1.1 for the example. The next line of the request is the host header. The host header was added to HTTP version 1.1 as a means to host multiple websites on a single IP address.

The server receiving this request verifies that it can service the request and then determines whether there is a resource called *devops.php* located in the document root. Assuming that the server is not too busy to handle the request, an HTTP response will be sent. If the file exists and the request was successful, the server begins responding with an HTTP status code of 200 and a reason phrase of OK. If an error occurred, then other status codes and reason phrases may be sent back, depending on the situation. For example, if there is no file called *devops.php* in the document root, then the server would respond with status code 404 and reason phrase of Not Found.

The other possible status codes are included in RFC 9110. A `GET` request may sometimes include a query string. A query string is a name-value pair that appears within the request after a question mark—for example:

```
GET /devops.php?date=20230803
```

In this example, the value `20230803` is sent to the server, which can act on that value, or not act on that value, depending on the contents of *devops.php*.

A request that uses the `POST` method looks largely the same as a `GET` request, although the request headers for `POST` will typically include Content-Length and Content-Type fields.

From the perspective of the DevSecOps practitioner, much of what happens with HTTP will be rather unimportant. However, when things go wrong, it is frequently because of a misconfigured server or because of a misunderstanding around protocol rules. For example, I once worked with a consulting firm that was designing a web application for my employer. Rather than use HTTP cookies and sessions, they placed session browsing information into the query string, which made it appear in the address bar of the browser. As a user navigated the application, the query string grew and grew. When deployed to production, real-world use cases of the application caused the query string to grow to over 10,000 characters and thus fail because that length was greater than that supported by most browsers.

When developing applications that face the web or utilize standard web browsers, developers are familiar with caching and the challenges surrounding cached JavaScript and Cascading Style Sheets. As with the TTL in DNS, the best that can be done is to ask the browser to not cache certain elements. It's up to the browser to honor the request. One brute-force method to avoid caching is to place a timestamp in the query string such that the browser believes it is requesting a new resource and thus won't evaluate the cache to use an old copy. The obvious implication of this practice is higher load on the server because it needs to service each request that might normally have been cached.

Other protocols

There are numerous other protocols that a DevSecOps practitioner will encounter during their career and even on a daily basis. Covering just two protocols, DNS and HTTP, leaves much room for additional learning on the part of the reader. The choice of DNS and HTTP was made purposefully based on career experience working with many levels of technical ability.

Even if I chose to cover six other protocols in depth, there will always be someone who will say, "What about..." for their favorite protocol. I read a lot of material on

Internetwork Packet Exchange/Sequenced Packet Exchange (IPX/SPX) networking in my early days of learning computing concepts. Even after it was clear that IP-based networks were here to stay, the IPX material was included in that material. While there's nothing wrong with IPX/SPX networks, including that material in books of the time was not a great use of trees.

With that in mind, rather than write specifically about several other protocols, I'll share a list of protocols that should be helpful for a DevSecOps practitioner to know:

File Transfer Protocol(s) (FTP)
FTP is not secure. Credentials and data are sent in the clear. Just the same, FTP is still used internally at many organizations. Knowing the differences between FTP, SFTP (Secure File Transfer Protocol), FTPS (FTP over SSL), and SCP (Secure Copy Protocol) would be useful knowledge, along with knowing which protocols your organization can support.

Secure Shell (SSH)
There is simultaneously much to learn and really not much to learn about SSH. Someone on a DevSecOps team will use SSH to configure servers remotely. Knowing how to use SSH keys and port forwarding would be quite helpful, but knowing the inner workings of the protocol itself is likely not necessary.

Knowing how to restart an SSH server safely from a remote location can save you hours of travel time.

Simple Network Management Protocol (SNMP)
You may never encounter SNMP, but the monitoring infrastructure that can appear within a DevSecOps team might use SNMP. Like SSH, there is everything to learn and not much to learn with SNMP.

Next, let's dig into some basics about data security.

Data Security: Confidentiality, Integrity, and Availability

The classic security triad includes confidentiality, integrity, and availability (CIA). When problems arise related to computer and data security, those problems can be traced back to one (or more) of the three. The person sitting next to you on the train, looking at your phone along with you, is violating the principle of confidentiality. Same for the eavesdropper, listening to a conversation of which they are not a participant.

Each layer of each protocol model described in the previous section represents an opportunity for an attack that violates one or more of confidentiality, integrity, and availability. Likewise, each layer represents a point at which security processes can be added or utilized to reduce the likelihood of an attack, mitigate the impact of an attack, or sometimes eliminate the attack entirely.

Of the three principles, confidentiality receives a significant amount of attention, likely due to the effects when confidentiality is lost. Integrity and availability are no less important. In particular, availability, or the lack thereof, is prominent in many ransomware attacks where data is encrypted and can only be unlocked with a secret key. Let's look at each principle in more detail:

Confidentiality

The examples earlier in this section, with a person looking at your phone or listening to your conversation, are trivial real-world situations where confidentiality is broken. Places like the United States do not typically have an expectation of privacy when in public locations, although shoulder-surfing someone's phone and similar issues may be handled differently depending on the situation. When indoors in a private space, there is an expectation of privacy.

Confidentiality applies to both data in transit and data at rest. Data in transit is typically thought of as data while it is traversing a network. Prior to the advent and ubiquity of WiFi, accessing large amounts of confidential data while in transit was significantly more difficult and involved gaining physical access to a facility through which the data passed.

Integrity

Contrast confidentiality, which is focused on others viewing data, with integrity, which is focused on ensuring that data is maintained in a known-good state. Unlike with confidentiality, there is no assumption that an attacker needs to view the data. Instead, merely being able to change the data itself is enough to violate integrity. For example, consider a scenario where the attacker can't see the result but is able to randomly flip bits within the data stream by overwhelming the receiver with fake traffic. The attacker can therefore randomly change things like results of a medical test or other important parts of the data being transferred or stored.

Availability

Availability, or the lack thereof, refers to situations where you cannot access or use computer systems, facilities, and data in the way that you would like to use them. This definition accounts for both physical attacks, where someone steals your laptop, and issues like a denial of service (DoS) attack, where computing services may be technically reachable but the performance is such that the service is effectively unusable for its intended purpose.

To the wider point of providing CIA, there is only so much that a member of the DevSecOps team can do to provide physical security or other elements required for ensuring security is maintained outside of the application development perspective. A starting point for those new to security concepts is the OWASP (Open Web Application Security Project) Top 10 (*https://owasp.org/www-project-top-ten*).

Though primarily focused on web applications, the OWASP Top 10 is a list of vulnerability categories that are commonly encountered by developers, operations personnel, and security analysts. The OWASP Top 10 includes things like broken authentication, cross-site scripting, insufficient logging, data exposure, and six others that may change by the time you read this. Anyone wishing to understand more about computer security, especially those tasked with creating applications, should find value in the OWASP categories—ideally, carrying that knowledge back to the application development process in ways that are specific to the languages and environment at their organization.

Chapter 3 provides more detailed information specific to each of the elements in the triad, and, like DevSecOps itself, coverage of issues related to security are integrated throughout the book. The next section transitions to a discussion of development as it relates to DevSecOps.

Development Overview for Scripting

The remainder of this chapter focuses on development constructs that will help lead toward scripting, or creation of small programs that perform one or more operations such as moving files, validating connectivity, or skimming logfiles. The goal is not to replace other learning opportunities or knowledge but rather to provide a starting point or stepping stone toward a deeper understanding of the concepts around programming.

A program is a series of instructions that cause the computer to perform an operation. At a very high level, a program is meant to solve a problem. In an organizational context, a program performs a business function. In many cases, the function could be performed without a computer. However, a computer can perform that function more efficiently, and thus the need to write a program. For example, taxes were calculated long before computers existed. However, computers can be programmed to make the calculation of taxes easier and more accurate.

From the highest level to the lowest, a computer processor relies on an instruction set that is used to perform the operations required by the higher-level program. In effect, developers can write their programs directly as instructions for the processor, or they can use a language that is then interpreted into the instruction set required by the processor. The concern in this book is around those higher-level programming languages.

PHP, JavaScript, Python, Perl, C++, and C are common higher-level programming languages that you might use today. In the case of languages like PHP and Python, you may write a full-stack web application or backend program, or you may write a smaller program.

This section specifically looks at the language components involved in creating a bash script. I assume that you have a shell environment available, specifically bash. If not, refer to "The Command-Line Interface" on page 18 for more details.

Commands and Built-ins

When working in the shell environment such as from the command line, you will use two elements: external commands and built-in commands. External commands are those that exist regardless of the shell program you're using. For example, the *cp* program is used to copy files. The *cp* program is usually located in the */bin* directory. If you're using bash, zsh, ash, tcsh, or some other shell, the *cp* program will be available for your use. When executed, the *cp* command creates a new process on the computer to complete its task.

Contrast the *cp* program, an external command, with a built-in command such as the *whence* command. The *whence* command provides information about how a shell will interpret a given command. For example, you would use *whence* to determine the location from which a command will execute. This helps to determine if the command is a built-in or an external command. In bash, the *whence* command has a *-t* option, but there is no *-t* option in zsh. Thus, a primary difference between an external command and a shell built-in is that the external command will work the same in all shell environments, whereas a built-in might not.

Basic Programmatic Constructs: Variables, Data, and Data Types

The goal of this section is to write a shell script. However, many of the concepts in this section are applicable to general programming irrespective of the language being used. In fact, some of the concepts will not work in bash.

When creating a program, more than likely that program will need to work with data of some variety. Variables are one means to store data for later use within a program. In bash, a variable is defined and assigned using the following syntax:

```
variable=value
```

For example, creating a variable called username containing the username of an account called rob would look like this:

```
username="rob"
```

Notice that there is no space between the name of the variable, the equals sign, and the value. Adding spaces will cause the script to fail.

Accessing variables in bash is accomplished by prepending a dollar sign onto the variable. For example, printing the contents of the username variable is done with the echo command and looks like this:

```
echo $username
```

 In Linux and macOS, a shell script is not executable by default. Rather, the file needs to have its execution bit set. Without getting into the complexities of Unix permissions, in the case of the example code, the command to add execute permissions for your user is chmod u+x <filename>, where <filename> is the name of the file being changed.

Variables are meant to hold data that might change. Contrast a variable with a constant. In programming terms, a constant is used to hold values that should never change throughout the lifetime of the application execution. An example is database credentials. While the software is running, the credentials should not change. Using a constant within the program has other benefits, like being able to inject the credentials from an outside source such as a configuration file. In bash, a constant is declared with the readonly built-in:

```
readonly username="rob"
```

Many languages use variables that can only hold one type of data, such as a number or a string of characters. Some languages are strongly typed, meaning that the language prevents variables from holding more than one sort of data. For example, a strongly typed language like Java requires that the programmer declare the type of variable, which can then never change. If a variable is declared to hold integers only, then it can never hold a string of characters.

Bash is not strongly typed. In fact, bash isn't typed at all. That means variables can hold a string or a number or anything else. The assumption is that the programmer knows what they are doing and intentionally changed the type of variable within the program. The requirement to program with intent is a topic for a different book. For the purposes of this book, when you create a variable to hold data, bash will allow you to change what that variable holds, should you need to do so.

Making Decisions with Conditionals

Some programs, especially scripts, will only need to perform a single operation where everything is known at the time of execution—for example, a bash script to create a backup or to import a comma-separated-value (CSV) file into a database. Even certain scripted programs will need to make decisions based on input or some external factor such as day of the week or time of day, weather condition, or something else that cannot be known when creating the program.

Conditionals are used to make decisions within programs. The if statement is a basic construct used for this purpose. An if statement evaluates whether or not a condition is true. If the condition is true, then the corresponding code executes. If the condition is not true, then the corresponding code does not execute.

Creating an if conditional with bash involves some of the more unique elements of bash when compared with other languages. In the program example, the username variable was created with a value of rob. If we wanted to take an action, such as print "Hello rob" based on that username, the code would look like this:

```
username="rob"
if [ $username == "rob" ]
then
    echo "Hello $username"
fi
```

Notice the new elements of syntax that are needed to create the conditional statement in bash. The if condition itself is enclosed within hard brackets. The comparison also uses double equals signs rather than a single equals sign. Although a single equals sign is valid in certain cases with bash, many languages only use the double-equals syntax, and thus to avoid confusion, I recommend using the double equals unless a compelling reason exists otherwise. To determine if a variable is not equal to, the ! operator is used, as in this example:

```
if [ $username != "rob" ]
then
    echo "Go Away"
fi
```

Bash comparison operators are special in that comparing numbers is accomplished using different terminology. Specifically, when comparing for equality for numeric values, the operator is -eq for equal and -ne for not equal. Various forms of greater than, less than, greater than or equal to, and less than or equal to use the two-letter syntax. The traditional greater than and less than signs, > and <, are used in bash, but those characters are used for comparing the sorting order of strings rather than for comparing numbers. Table 2-1 shows common operators in bash.

Table 2-1. Common operators in bash

Operator	Description
==	Compare strings for equality
!=	Negation, or not equal, for strings
>	Compare sort order of strings, greater than
<	Compare sort order of strings, less than
-eq	Equal, for numbers
-ne	Not equal, for numbers

Operator	Description
-lt	Less than, for numbers
-gt	Greater than, for numbers
-le	Less than or equal to, for numbers
-ge	Greater than or equal to, for numbers

Bash also includes several operators to test the properties of files and directories, as shown in Table 2-2. These operators are quite useful in the context of bash scripting because of the frequent use of bash scripts to solve filesystem-related issues.

Table 2-2. Select operators in bash

Operator	Description
-d	Tests if the file is a directory
-e	Tests if the file exists
-f	Tests if the file is a regular file and not a directory or special file
-r	Evaluates whether the user running the test has read permission on the file
-w	Evaluates whether the user running the test has write permission on the file
-x	Evaluates whether the user running the test has execute permission on the file

Numerous other file tests exist and are described in the Advanced Bash-Scripting Guide (*https://tldp.org/LDP/abs/html/fto.html*).

Thus far, coverage of conditionals has been limited to the if statement. However, bash and other languages also provide a means for executing code if the test fails by means of an else condition. A real-world example: if the temperature is greater than 85 degrees (Fahrenheit), then wear shorts, else wear pants.

The else condition provides code that will execute if the primary test fails. But what if you need to perform more than one test? You can use the elif statement to perform another test. Carrying on with the weather example: if the temperature is greater than 85 degrees, then wear shorts, else if the temperature is greater than 50 degrees then wear pants, else wear pants and bring a jacket. In code:

```
if [ $temperature -gt 85 ]
then
    echo "Wear shorts"
elif [ $temperature -gt 50 ]
then
    echo "Wear pants"
else
    echo "Wear pants and bring a jacket"
```

After a few `if`/`elif` combinations, code can be somewhat more cumbersome to troubleshoot and maintain. Bash and other languages have a `case` statement that enables several options to be evaluated efficiently and an execution path chosen based on the result of the evaluation. `case` or `case/switch` will not be covered further in this book. See *Bash Guide for Beginners* (*https://tldp.org/LDP/Bash-Beginners-Guide/html/sect_07_03.html*) for more information.

Looping

Thus far, I've covered using variables to store data within a program, as well as making decisions within the code on which path to execute based on the contents of those variables or other tests. Next up is looping, or performing the same operation more than once.

Most languages include at least two means for looping, with several other ways available depending on the language. Bash includes both a `for` loop and a `while` loop along with its closely related cousin, an `until` loop.

The `for` loop iterates through a block of code a certain number of times, where that number depends on the need of the program. The `for` loop is frequently used to iterate over a list of items, performing an operation on each item in the list. Here is a `for` loop that uses a list of files and provides output if the file is a regular file as opposed to a directory or special character device or similar:

```
files=$( ls )
for file in $files
do
  if [ -f "$file" ]
  then
    echo "$file is a regular file"
  fi
done
```

Within the example code, there is a new element that we haven't covered yet. The first line of the code assigns the output from the `ls` command to a variable within the script. There are other methods for capturing output, including enclosing the command in run quotes, or ` ` (also known as backticks). The syntax shown, `$( )`, can be helpful for cases where spaces may be involved in the output, like filenames gathered with `ls`.

A `while` loop iterates through a block of code only when a condition remains true. If the condition isn't true to begin with, the `while` loop will never execute the code within. The `until` loop is like the `while` loop except that the code will only be executed when a condition remains false. If the condition is true to begin with, then the code within the `until` loop will never execute.

You may hear the term DRY, or Don't Repeat Yourself. The DRY principle is intended as a reminder to avoid repetitive code or the same block of code in multiple locations in a program. While not exactly related to looping, when the DRY principle is violated, code becomes more difficult to maintain.

Consider the example of code to calculate sales tax. The same calculation may need to be performed in multiple places in the code. If something changes about how the tax needs to be calculated, the developer tasked with making the change needs to find all of the locations where that same code exists.

Lists and Arrays

In the previous section, a list of files was gathered by running the `ls` command. Lists are another commonly used programmatic construct. Lists may also be called arrays, and sometimes you might hear lists referred to as dictionaries or by other similar terms. Lists, arrays, and dictionaries differ, but those differences are beyond the scope of this book. Consider a list to be a simpler form of an array in bash, and the previous section showed a common creation and use of a list. Arrays in bash can be numerically indexed or indexed by a string, also called an associative array or dictionary. As you read through more examples later in the book, the use of arrays and lists will become more evident.

Summary

This chapter provided an overview of several concepts relevant to people and organizations moving toward DevSecOps. The coverage was intentionally broad, as it is impossible to fully cover all of the necessary foundational concepts in just 25 pages or even in 250 pages. Entire books have been written about subsections of this chapter alone. My hope, then, was to enable you to at least have some sense of the broad knowledge base needed for a DevSecOps practitioner. Just as with playing a musical instrument, the more you practice, the more you will add both depth and breadth to the skills needed in all three areas: development, security, and operations.

The chapter began with an appeal to learn the command line regardless of operating system. For years to come, learning the command line, especially a Unix-based command line like Linux or macOS, will help you to automate tasks and gain speed in day-to-day work. Ports and protocols were covered next in the chapter, with a look at the OSI and internet models for representing communication. Protocol coverage included DNS and HTTP, focusing especially on DNS and HTTP as base-level protocols that should just work but sometimes don't.

Next I introduced the security triad of confidentiality, integrity, and availability (CIA)—though much security coverage is found in Chapter 3. Finally, with the programmatic constructs section, the goal was simply to introduce the reader to key-words around programming. Noting the centrality of bash scripting for DevSecOps, much focus was around examples in bash, but the same programmatic constructs exist in many other languages today.

The focus of Chapter 3 is foundational security knowledge. The chapter includes coverage of the basic CIA triad and related security concepts with the goal of infusing those concepts across the development lifecycle. The chapter also shows some hands-on tooling with OWASP.

Integrating Security

Chapter 2 provided some of the foundational aspects for establishing the technical skills related to DevSecOps, including a brief introduction to the security triad of confidentiality, integrity, and availability (CIA). This chapter adds depth around those three concepts. The chapter begins with an overview of security practice integration and wraps up with a hands-on practical implementation related to security through a demonstration of the OWASP ZAP tool.

Integrating Security Practices

In DevSecOps, security is an integral element contained within each step of the software development lifecycle. Importantly, rather than having a single team dedicated to security, the processes and tools are available to and used by all members of a DevSecOps team. This section examines security practices in the context of DevSecOps. It begins with the concept of least privilege and then circles back to issues around CIA. The section does not cover every computer security practice and tool. Specifically not included in this section are items that any organization should be doing already, regardless of their stance on DevSecOps. For example, the following is an inexhaustive list of processes and tools that should exist regardless of DevSecOps:

- Patch and update process should be well-established and implemented.
- Threat modeling and identification of attack vectors and attack surface should be ongoing.
- Smart and useful security training should have been implemented where needed.
- Compliance has been ensured for relevant legal and regulatory requirements.

- Disaster recovery policies have been implemented.
- Incident response and recovery should be based on best practices.

The CIA triad provides a base that you can refer to when considering options around processes and technologies for DevSecOps. It is possible to map key concepts in DevSecOps to one or more of the three elements of the triad:

- Implementing least privilege → confidentiality, integrity, availability
- Role-based authentication → confidentiality, integrity, availability
- Visibility and security testing → confidentiality, integrity, availability
- Using key- and certificate-based authentication → confidentiality, integrity, availability
- Code traceability → confidentiality, integrity
- Establishing decommissioning processes → confidentiality

Let's dig into the idea of implementing least privilege.

Implementing Least Privilege

In my role as advisor for the campus radio station, I have many physical keys. There are so many keys that I keep them on multiple keyrings, which is to say that I have one keyring for normal days and then a gigantic ring of rings containing enough keys to make a locksmith jealous. Even with all of those keys, I can't get into every building and room on campus. I don't need to do so. I have the minimum number of keys required for my role, enabling me to have the least amount of access needed to accomplish the tasks involved in the job. This is the concept of least privilege.

Applying this to the concept of computing, it isn't necessary for everyone to have full administrator privileges on every server or even on their own computer. Certain software will require elevated privileges in order to be installed, but beyond the installation, day-to-day work doesn't require a higher level of access. Least privilege can be frustrating at times, because of the context switching required when a developer finds that they can't access certain data. Least privilege can also be helpful when data goes missing or a server is misconfigured because the individuals who don't have permission can't be the ones who deleted the data!

In practical terms, granting the minimum rights needed for database users is one easy method for implementing least privilege. For example, if the user connecting to the database only needs to read (select) data, then there is no reason to grant the ability to update or delete data. Likewise, if the user only needs to create new records, then privileges for viewing data or deleting data should not be granted.

Setting file and directory access in Linux

Though additional variations exist like setuid/setgid, on a day-to-day basis there are three levels of access and three permissions that can be granted for file and directory permissions on a Linux system. The three levels are user, group, and other. The "other" in this case is sometimes also referred to as "world." Permissions applied to "other" apply separately from user and group permissions. If you'd like more information on the other uses of chmod, see its manual page. "Basic Command-Line Navigation" on page 163 in Appendix B provides more information about the manual pages in Linux.

The three permissions are read, write, and execute. For example, a user would typically have read and write privileges on a text file within their home directory on a Linux system, whereas those in the same group or elsewhere on the server may have the ability to read but not write to the file. Group permissions and "other" permissions can be set separately and control access differently than for the user.

You can change permissions with the chmod command in Linux using a numeric octal format or letter-based format known as symbolic notation. In octal notation, the number 4 represents read privileges, 2 represents write, and 1 represents execute. In symbolic notation, r represents read, w represents write, and x represents execute. This is shown in Table 3-1.

Table 3-1. Linux permission system

Octal	Symbolic Letter	Description
4	r	Read
2	w	Write
1	x	Execute

When assigning permissions with a three-digit octal notation, the user is the first number, the group is the second, and other is the third. For example, assigning read privileges to all users on a file called *data.txt* looks like this:

```
chmod 444 data.txt
```

The octal notation is additive, meaning that assigning the ability for the user to read and write but group and other to only read is 644, as in this example:

```
chmod 644 data.txt
```

With symbolic notation, the user is represented by the letter u, group is represented by g, other is represented by o, and all three are represented by a letter a. Effecting the same 644 permissions with symbolic notation would be:

```
chmod u+rw,go+r data.txt
```

Whether you choose numeric or symbolic depends on the need or situation in which you're making the change. For example, it may be easier programmatically to use octal permissions because of the special characters needed (the plus sign and comma) when using symbolic notation.

This entire section thus far has been a lead-in to preventing you from invoking a solution that you will sometimes see on the internet: adding read, write, and execute permission for the world, the infamous "777" permission. With the knowledge that you have from this section, you now know that granting everyone the ability to read, write, and execute a data file almost certainly violates the concept of least privilege and will make accountability more difficult as well. It is exceedingly rare that chmod 777 is the correct solution, and if a vendor or consultant recommends 777 as a solution, then it's time to find a new vendor or consultant.

Role-based access control (RBAC)

The concepts of least privilege and role-based access control (RBAC) work together to make management easier while improving security. RBAC can be thought of as group-based permissions. At a higher level, RBAC is the process of granting permissions based on the role or job duties. For example, a new developer has different responsibilities than the person who hired them. The role of hiring manager necessitates access to data about the candidates, salaries, and other details that someone hired into a developer role wouldn't need to do their job. Therefore, the access control needs are different for the two individuals.

Managing permissions based on roles saves significant time versus granting permissions to individuals. When those individuals change roles or leave the company, someone must go through each data element and system to make sure that the permissions have been revoked. With RBAC, the person only needs to be removed from nonessential groups, which then alleviates the need to work through every system.

Maintaining Confidentiality

It is necessary to maintain confidentiality of data at several levels. First, while data is at rest or in storage, it needs to be protected. This is true whether that data is stored as files on a disk or stored as files in a filing cabinet. It is also necessary to protect data while it travels between storage and use. Like the at-rest protection, in-flight protection for data includes electronic transactions such as visiting a bank web page but also instances when the data is being physically moved such as with an offsite backup. Finally, data in use is another level within which data must be protected.

Data in Flight

Among the most common methods for protecting confidentiality with computer systems is encryption. Secure Sockets Layer (SSL) or Transport Layer Security (TLS) provides encryption for transactions on the web. The *https://* protocol scheme is an indicator that an SSL/TLS connection is being used for the communication between a client web browser and a server. With HTTPS connections, an attacker can view the traffic, but the contents of that traffic will be encrypted.

You might think of this as mailing a letter versus mailing a postcard. When you mail a postcard, anyone who has access to the postcard can view not only who sent the postcard and the details of the intended recipient but also the contents of the postcard. If you're vacationing in Hawaii and send a postcard back to your relatives in snowy Wisconsin, all of the postal workers between Hawaii and Wisconsin can see that you're having a great time and read about your beach adventures. There's nothing particularly confidential about those details.

Contrast a letter being sent in an envelope from Hawaii to Wisconsin. The postal worker can see the sender and the recipient but nothing more. For now, it's OK to ignore the ability to look through the envelope or even open the letter. Instead, assume that the letter is enclosed in a security envelope and that the postal worker is less interested in your mail because it's easier and more enjoyable to view postcards.

When using standard HTTP, without the "S," the request, response, and the data itself can be viewed by anyone in between the HTTP server and the client making the request. In practical terms, anyone on the same WiFi network could see this traffic. In that scenario, the WiFi network being eavesdropped is equivalent to the postal worker, and the HTTP request is equivalent to the postcard. When a form of encryption is added, the transaction becomes more like mailing a letter. While the eavesdropper can see the traffic and some elements of the request, they cannot see the contents or data of that traffic.

Adding the ability to peek inside the network traffic while it is traversing the network, even if that traffic is encrypted, is the equivalent of the postal worker seeing through or opening the envelope. Vulnerabilities have been found in the protocols used to protect HTTP traffic. Notably, the Heartbleed attack (*https://cve.mitre.org/cgi-bin/cvename.cgi?name=cve-2014-0160*) from the early 2010s enabled attackers to view traffic destined for web servers that used certain versions of software meant to protect the transactions. The problems went undetected for several months. The equivalent would be not only opening an envelope but steaming the envelope open and then resealing it. With no reason to believe otherwise, the recipient would open the envelope just like normal.

DNS over HTTPS Breaks the Internet

Confidentiality goes beyond the opportunity to eavesdrop or capture data. Recall from Chapter 2 that requests for web pages or other resources typically use a friendly name rather than an IP address. When the request involves a name, a name-to-IP lookup takes place. Normally this lookup is done through a DNS (Domain Name System) request that is sent by the client to a DNS resolver. This is illustrated in Figure 3-1.

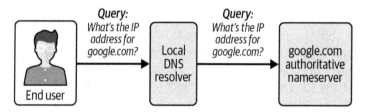

Figure 3-1. A DNS lookup to a local DNS resolver that ends up being sent to an authoritative name server

For home users, typically a broadband customer, their consumer-level router obtains a list of IP addresses of DNS resolvers from their internet service provider (ISP). These DNS resolvers, more commonly called DNS servers, are located at the internet provider. When a computer, phone, or other device performs a DNS lookup, the request eventually ends up at the DNS server operated by the ISP. The effect of using this path for DNS resolution is that the ISP can see and log the DNS requests coming from each customer who uses the ISP's DNS servers. The ISP then has a view into the browsing habits and usage of its customers, even for connections and protocols that are otherwise secure, like HTTPS.

DNS over HTTPS (DoH) uses centralized DNS resolvers to perform lookups. In this way, the resolution no longer occurs at the ISP level but rather at the centralized set of DNS servers chosen by large tech companies such as Google and Apple. The premise is to prevent the ISP from seeing the DNS request. However, not only does DoH merely move the privacy implications to a central location, but the word "centralization" is anathema to the decentralized design of the internet. Rather than DNS requests being spread among the ISPs, those DNS requests can now be easily combined with other browsing habits at a central or aggregated location. Worse yet, DoH also operates over TCP, thus requiring more resources and generally being slower than a standard DNS request.

Eavesdropping on email

Simple Mail Transfer Protocol (SMTP) is the default, unencrypted means for email to be exchanged between servers on the internet. The effect of email being unencrypted means that anyone who can interject themselves between two SMTP servers can view all of the email messages being sent between those servers. While it is certainly plausible for an eavesdropper to place themselves in the right spot to obtain email, both the difficulty in gaining access to interject themselves without being detected and the sheer amount of storage required to effectively sift through those email messages makes this attack vector less likely than others. In addition, the increasing use of encrypted SMTP exchanges further reduces the attack surface of SMTP.

The same vulnerability (of being unencrypted) exists for the two primary email retrieval protocols, POP3 (Post Office Protocol v3) and IMAP (Internet Message Access Protocol). Both POP3 and IMAP are unencrypted. There is a greater chance of an attacker being able to view messages with POP3 and IMAP, though the scale is smaller. Like HTTP, the attacker can interject themselves by eavesdropping on the same WiFi network.

Ideally, the attacker would eavesdrop from a location that contains a lot of email. The same difficulties that apply to SMTP also apply to eavesdropping on POP3 and IMAP at a large scale. The attacker needs to gain access, avoid detection, and have enough capacity to store the emails. You might think of this as the *Ocean's Eleven* (2001 version) scenario. The team needs to gain access to the vault, avoid detection, and then somehow get a significant amount of money out.

SMTP, POP3, and IMAP can all be encrypted by adding or integrating SSL/TLS into the mix. It's likely that your email is encrypted between you and the server on which it is stored, and sometimes the exchange of that email will also be encrypted between servers. As with HTTP, a successful attack against the encryption means that the attacker gains full access to the traffic being exchanged.

Other protocols use encryption for keeping the contents of the traffic away from eavesdroppers. Secure Shell (SSH) is a widely used protocol for data transfer and remote administration. Data exchanged with SSH is encrypted. An encryption layer can also be added onto File Transfer Protocol (FTP), making it more difficult for an attacker to view the data being exchanged.

Wired versus WiFi versus offline

The mode of transport also matters for data while it is moving. Data that traverses a network from end to end on wires is less susceptible to eavesdropping than data that travels wirelessly at any point. In this context, wirelessly can mean anything from WiFi to cellular/LTE to radio to carrier pigeon (see RFC 1149 (*https:// datatracker.ietf.org/doc/html/rfc1149*)). Wireless communication enables an attacker to eavesdrop without exerting much effort, with an exception being point-to-point wireless communication—where some effort would need to be exerted but not nearly the same as trying to eavesdrop on a wired network.

As related to both the OSI and IP models shown in Chapter 2, both Ethernet and WiFi are represented at the physical layer. The physical layer is tangible and visible when holding an Ethernet cable, and the attacks on the physical layer are evident if you apply a sharp pair scissors to the Ethernet cable. A single cut of the cable is enough to make any connected devices become unavailable.

WiFi is more difficult to visualize and is impossible to cut with scissors. WiFi networks use radio waves to communicate, just like FM and AM radio, TV, satellites, cellular phones and data, and other forms of wireless communication. The frequencies vary from technology to technology, which explains why you don't get cellular signals on an FM radio but also why running a microwave oven can sometimes affect other nearby signals like cordless phones and older WiFi. Microwave ovens operate around 2,450 megahertz (MHz), which is within the range used by WiFi.

WiFi and cellular data are both encrypted, or more accurately, WiFi traffic can be encrypted. Like encryption applied to a wired connection, the encryption on WiFi and cellular does not prevent eavesdropping. Rather, the encryption raises the cost to access useful data within the encrypted packets. Assuming other vulnerabilities do not exist, the attacker needs to capture the traffic and then decrypt it.

Wireless communication lowers the cost of capturing the traffic, but upper-layer protocols remain in place to encrypt the data as well. For example, even if the attacker can break the encryption of the wireless communication, they must still decrypt the HTTP traffic protected by SSL/TLS. The related methods for obtaining information through DNS requests still exist and can also reveal information that violates user confidentiality.

A final instance where data needs to be protected while in transit is when that data is stored on a physical medium and that physical medium is being transported or moved. Backup media are an example where data is being transported and might be stolen while in transport. If the data on the backup media is not encrypted, then it will be fully available to the attacker, assuming they have hardware that is appropriate to connect the media.

Data at Rest

Thus far, the focus has been on data while "in flight," or being sent through the network, with a special case noted when the data is stored on a physical medium and is being physically transported from one location to another. The data itself is being transferred in aggregate form but is also "at rest" or in storage, such as on a backup tape, USB drive, or other format.

Files and databases stored on a hard drive or other form of storage are also subject to vulnerabilities that could compromise the confidentiality of that data. An attacker may download an entire database while it is online, or a thief may physically steal the hard drives or other media, both of which increase the scale and potential impact of the compromised data.

When an attacker obtains a database, they have the ability to examine all of its contents at once. Contrast this to in-flight compromises, where the attacker may gain access to many transactions but then must filter those transactions to find the interesting traffic. Rather than a transaction-based compromise, stealing data at rest often enables the attacker to sell large amounts of data in aggregate form.

A primary means to mitigate the risk from such a compromise is database-level encryption. Like SSL and other encrypted means of communication, encrypting data at rest will usually stop an attacker from obtaining the actual data. At the least, encryption will act as a delay while the attacker works to decrypt the contents. There is an implication that the encryption is of a reasonably strong cipher as opposed to an obfuscation or a cipher created by someone within the organization who is simply good at math.

As with SSL/TLS encryption, using standard ciphers such as Advanced Encryption Standard (AES) comes with a risk that there is a known means to quickly and cost-effectively decipher the contents. Rumors of state actors having such backdoors do exist, but there is little, if any, proof of the same. Regardless, a targeted attack with significant resources may be able to simply brute-force the encryption.

Therefore, while it's good to know that these problems exist, those problems should not prevent you from using database- or file-level encryption when possible. Knowing that a door lock can be picked by a skilled locksmith isn't sufficient reason for leaving the door open. Thinking around locks, there is another line of thinking around encryption.

Envision a scenario in a particularly dangerous parking lot. A would-be thief is walking through the parking lot randomly testing car doors to see if they are unlocked. When the doors are unlocked, the potential thief simply moves on to the next vehicle under the premise that there must not be anything of value in the car if the owner left the doors unlocked. If the car doors are locked, efforts are made to unlock the car or otherwise simply brute-force their way in with a brick through the door window. If the owner locked the car doors, then there must be something of value.

Likewise, if an attacker finds encrypted files and/or data, they may increase their efforts to decrypt on the basis that there must be something valuable inside simply because the data is encrypted. The key difference between this and the car door scenario is that the attacker has already gained at least some access in order to get to the encrypted files. Ultimately, if the encryption is sufficiently strong and it becomes obvious that the attacker will need to expend significant resources to access the unencrypted contents, there is a good chance that they will move to the next target.

The fundamental problem is that computers get faster and vulnerabilities become available in the ciphers themselves. This decreases the cost of decrypting the data. This is less of a concern for time-sensitive data that would not have value if deciphered in 10 years but is problematic for long-lived data like Social Security numbers and medical records.

Verifying Integrity

Maintaining and verifying integrity is somewhat more difficult or cumbersome to accomplish than maintaining confidentiality and availability. To maintain integrity implies there is or was a verifiable source of original truth from which a given bit of data can be verified. The verifiability of the original source of truth is a key element. As an attacker, if I can change both the integrity of data and the source of verification, then there will not be a method for verifying integrity. Even worse, because the verification source now matches the data that I maliciously changed, the problem may not be found immediately, if at all. Such is the difficulty with maintaining integrity.

Checksums

Checksums or one-way hashes are a common method to verify integrity. Take a data file or random string of characters on a computer and execute a hash function on it, returning the hashed string. The string of characters returned provides a fingerprint of the input, essentially a string of characters that represent the input data. The fingerprint can be used as a means to determine if the current data file has been altered from its original, assuming that a fingerprint was taken of the original file and that the fingerprint itself has been kept secure. Figure 3-2 shows a file with the phrase "file with super secret data" along with the hash as produced by the sha256sum command.

Figure 3-2. A file checksum is a unique value based on the contents of the file

Notice what happens to the hash when the letter "f" in "file" is changed to an uppercase "F," shown in Figure 3-3.

Figure 3-3. A file checksum; compare to Figure 3-2, noting that the file contents have changed

By changing a single letter, the hash produced by sha256sum is completely different. Seeing this would indicate that something has changed within the file, though it is not proof of malice. There are many reasons a file might change, including normal use but also disk errors and other anomalies.

It's worth noting that changing the uppercase "F" back to lowercase "f" in the word file from the previous example also then changes the hash value back to its original. The hashing functions used to verify integrity do not verify or validate that the file has not been temporarily changed and then put back in place or back to its original state.

The examples shared in this section show the sha256sum hash function being executed on a small, 28-byte file. Hash functions also work on larger files and perform the same operation. While it's not obvious from the 28-byte example here, the hash produced by sha256sum when run against a multigigabyte file will also produce a 64-byte hexadecimal string. The term "one-way" that is sometimes associated with hash functions means that it is impossible to re-create the source file by using the hash value itself.

In practice, one-way hash functions provide a data point in the integrity verification process. While it's difficult to obtain the same hash value from two different files, collisions do occur, and there is no guarantee of a fingerprint being globally unique. Additionally, the hash functions themselves can be broken or altered in such a way to cause the fingerprint to be the same. Attackers will also use malicious programs in place of the normal hash function programs, thus causing their files to pass the hash fingerprint tests.

Many software vendors provide checksums as a means to verify that the file you downloaded is the original, trusted copy of that file. For example, Microsoft currently provides SHA256 values for downloads of Windows 10. However, if attackers gain access to critical infrastructure, they can (and will) not only replace the source files with their own versions but also replace the valid checksum values with their own. Thus, even if you take the step of verifying the checksum, you can still receive malicious software.

Hash functions have evolved as computers have become more powerful and as methods to attack hash functions have become widely known. Message digest–based hash functions had been used until recently when Secure Hashing Algorithm–based functions became more widely used. It is common to see the hash values produced with the SHA256 algorithm today, but that may change to SHA512 or some other algorithm by the time you're reading this.

 Further depth of coverage around hashing algorithms and cryptographic strength is beyond the scope of this book. Further reading can be found in Bruce Schneier's book *Applied Cryptography* (Wiley, 2015), among others.

Both key-based and certificate-based authentication can be used to remove the ability for an attacker to guess or brute-force a password. Rather than prompting for a password, a client presents a certificate that was signed by a certificate authority (CA) that is trusted by the server. For example, the SSH protocol is used extensively in DevSecOps processes for remote administration and file transfer. The OpenSSH implementation of the protocol can use various forms of authentication, including key-based and certificate-based. With certificate-based authentication, a CA is created and each SSH server then trusts certificates signed by that CA. Key-based authentication is similar insofar as configuration needs to be performed on the server to establish the trust relationship to accept the key that is presented. There is additional overhead with key-based authentication, but in terms of DevSecOps, the process for key distribution will be automated regardless of whether key- or certificate-based authentication is used. The specific advantage to certificate-based authentication is that the necessary OpenSSH configuration can be distributed when the environment is being built.

Verifying Email

A few technologies help to facilitate verification of the source of emails: SPF, DKIM, and DMARC. Sender Policy Framework (SPF) provides a way to indicate that emails for a given domain should only originate from certain IP addresses. For example, an SPF record can be created to indicate that the IP address 10.4.2.65 is the only valid IP from which emails claiming to be from *example.com* can originate. If an email claiming to be from *example.com* arrives from a different IP address, then it can be considered invalid.

DomainKeys Identified Mail (DKIM) is another method for helping to validate that an email was sent from the sender that claims to have sent it. Whereas SPF provides indication of the valid IPs that can send email for a domain, DKIM uses public-key cryptography to add a digital signature of the sender to the email. The receiving server can verify the digital signature originates from the sending domain server through a DNS record.

Both SPF and DKIM can be used as data points in helping to determine the validity of a message. Like checksums for files, SPF and DKIM are subject to various vulnerabilities, and thus verification accomplished or rejected because of SPF and DKIM should be considered one of many facets that indicate the message is valid or invalid.

DMARC, or Domain-based Message Authentication, Reporting, and Conformance, works in conjunction with both SPF and DKIM to provide message handling and reporting capabilities. Like SPF and DKIM, DMARC uses a DNS record to help validate the From header (RFC 5322) and signal what to do if the message is not valid, such as reject the message or quarantine it. With the combination of DMARC, SPF, and DKIM, the attack vector of phishing becomes more challenging but not impossible.

SPF, DKIM, and DMARC rely on DNS to function. As an attacker, knowing that DNS records create a single point of failure for SPF, DKIM, and DMARC, successfully exploiting an organization's DNS infrastructure enables me to add an extra authorized IP for SPF, change the DKIM signature to one of my own, or change the policy for DMARC.

DNS also provides an interesting attack surface for other records that could affect integrity as well. There are numerous examples of attackers successfully transferring domains away from their rightful owner through any number of shady tactics. But even if the attacker doesn't steal the entire domain, simply being able to log in to a DNS control panel and change records or being able to spoof DNS responses enables the attacker to create a man-in-the-middle (MITM) attack.

Providing Availability

Availability is a broad subject encompassing both the virtual and physical realms. Availability means ensuring that the system is available when needed and at the expected performance level. This necessitates identifying single points of failure and then taking steps to provide redundancy for those points of failure. Sometimes the costs of eliminating a single point of failure is simply too high, and the organization needs to accept the risk. Space launches are a prime example. Aside from building two or three of everything, the risk of catastrophic failure must be accepted at certain times.

At other times, the cost of providing availability can be shifted. Organizations can avoid capital investments for redundant data centers and provide physical security for those data centers by utilizing cloud-based deployments. The cost of providing availability for computing has decreased with the advent of automated cloud deployment capabilities. Applications can be deployed across multiple cloud providers and across multiple regions of the world such that if one cloud provider has a problem or there is a natural disaster affecting a data center, the load for that application can be shifted to another provider in another part of the world instantly and automatically.

Service-Level Agreements and Service-Level Objectives

A service-level agreement (SLA) may exist between an organization and its providers. The SLA dictates how much downtime is acceptable during a given period, such as a month, a quarter, or a year. The criteria for determining acceptable service is also included in an SLA. A simple ping to indicate server availability will miss scenarios where the web server is too busy to handle HTTP requests.

An SLA may also exist internally, with the technology department needing to provide a certain level of service to business function departments. An SLA may use a service-level objective (SLO) for each service. At other times, you may hear the term "service-level objective" instead of the more formalized connotation of an agreement. An SLO has the same goal as an SLA: to create an understanding of when a service will be available.

Defining an SLA involves several steps:

1. Identify stakeholders who require the system to be available.
2. Identify needs around uptime or availability of the system.
3. Define availability.
4. Estimate costs for providing the requested uptime.

Let's dig into each of these steps in more detail.

Identifying Stakeholders

At times, stakeholder identification is straightforward. The users of the application are stakeholders, and those who paid for the application to be developed or paid for using the application are stakeholders. A modern web application will have numerous stakeholders. In some cases, stakeholders are not directly represented, such as with a public website where users don't have a direct influence on decisions about the application or its availability. Some methods for addressing this deficiency include utilizing user groups or representatives from the internal customer service department who work with end users and can represent the needs of the users.

Identifying Availability Needs

Stakeholders can provide information on when the system is used. This information can be gathered through interviews/meetings and through observation. Of the two, interviews and observation, the latter is more accurate as to how and when the system is being used. Regardless of whether interviews or observation is used, you should also gather supplemental information through system usage logs. This may be network-related traffic logs or request logs for a web server. You may gather information through interviews and observation only to find something new in the system logs that requires another round of interviews.

Seasonal or cyclical activities may also be missed and should be incorporated as part of any interview or log analysis exercise for identifying availability needs of a system. For example, a monthly reconciliation activity that runs overnight on the last day of the month might not be thought of by stakeholders during interviews and wouldn't be observed. If you choose an availability level that included only normal business hours, then this process may be adversely affected by downtime.

Defining Availability and Estimating Costs

Availability of a system exists from the perspective of the user of that system. But what does "availability" mean? Is responding to a ping sufficient evidence of availability, or does the service need to respond at the protocol level, such as by serving an HTTP request? What time interval is acceptable for a response time—subseconds, seconds, minutes? That answer depends on the system and process.

Monitoring software is able to examine various metrics to determine availability. Some software, like Prometheus, requires software to be installed on the device to be monitored. Other software, like Zabbix and Icinga, can use SSH to run commands on the client device. There are also proprietary solutions for monitoring. Rather than attempting to be prescriptive or choosing one over another, you can use the criteria in Table 3-2 when considering monitoring software solutions.

Table 3-2. Evaluation criteria for monitoring software

Criteria	Description
Protocols to be monitored	What protocols can be monitored? Are there specific checks for higher-level protocols like HTTP, SSH, and others, along with TCP, UDP, ICMP?
Complexity of checks	Assuming that an HTTP check is going to be used, can the software look for text on the page and also provide metrics for response time?
Additional monitoring	Can the software monitor host both compute resources and network devices (such as with SNMP)?
Dependency monitoring	Can the software create host and service dependencies, such as making sure an outbound gateway connection is available prior to marking services as being down?
Agentless monitoring	Does the software require additional client software to be installed on each device, or can it utilize standard protocols and commands for monitoring?
Limited access	Whether or not an agent is required on the client, is the client portion able to work with limited access/least privilege rather than needing administrator/root privileges on the client?
Alerting flexibility	Are there multiple methods for sending alerts such that escalations can be defined and acknowledgments can be sent back while a problem is being corrected?

Criteria	Description
Scaling	How does the monitoring software perform at scale? Is there an upper limit of services and hosts that can be monitored, or can the monitoring software itself be deployed in ways to spread the monitoring load?
Performance metrics	Does the software store data in such a way that multiple types of performance reports can be defined, created, and gathered, or are the reports already defined?
Monitoring redundancy	Can the software work in a redundant manner, such that more than one instance of the monitoring software can be deployed in case the primary monitoring resources become unavailable?
Open source	Is the source code normally available for viewing, whether or not licensed under a "free" license?
Export of data	Can monitoring and performance data be exported easily and in a standard format such that it can be consumed by other systems for reporting or other purposes?

Defining availability leads directly to enhanced monitoring of systems along with identification of intermediary systems and single points of failure. A single point of failure is a component that, if missing or unavailable, causes the entire system to break down. For example, having three web servers in a load-balanced configuration provides redundancy for web requests. Should something happen to web server 1, then web servers 2 and 3 can handle the load while web server 1 is repaired. However, in the configuration depicted in Figure 3-4, there is only one load balancer. Thus, the load balancer itself represents a single point of failure. If the load balancer has a problem, then all requests are stopped.

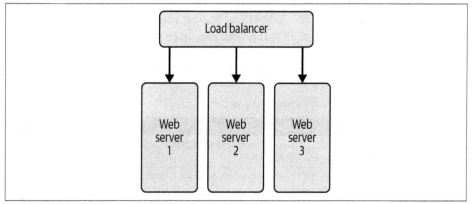

Figure 3-4. A load balancer as a single point of failure

Cost estimation can be accomplished in several ways, depending on how an organization handles overhead costs such as building and facilities. For some organizations, each square foot of a building will be accounted for internally and a cost factor associated with it. For example, if the marketing department uses 30% of the space in the building, then 30% of the costs associated with operating the building will be allocated as a cost to the marketing budget. As redundancy and SLAs/SLOs are being considered, if additional space is needed for a redundant data center, then there may be additional hidden costs such as those internal operational costs. Again, how operational costs are allocated is handled differently between organizations. When using cloud-based resources to meet SLA/SLO goals, such internal overhead costs will be minimized.

Regardless of internal allocations, meeting certain levels of performance becomes increasingly costly as additional levels of performance are desired.

At times, the costs to provide the requested level of uptime will be prohibitive. A customer may request 24/7/365 uptime for an application that is really only used during business hours. Therefore, patching and updating along with backup creation could be done after business hours. The "five nines" of uptime, or 99.999% uptime, requires less than six minutes of downtime per year. That level of service is possible, but it will be much more costly than a business-hours performance objective.

What About Accountability?

In the context of this chapter, accountability refers to being able to track who, what, and when—in other words, being able to provide the answer to the questions "Who did what, and when did they do it?" In computing, the answer is found through activity logging.

Prior to *systemd*, logging on to a Linux server was accomplished in plain text files, usually located in */var/log*. This system, also known as *syslog*, was well documented and easy to use but had some challenges when scaled up. Server administrators could script many solutions based on the contents of logfiles, monitor the logfiles in real time, import log entries into a database, and automatically archive old logs. *Systemd* ruined the simplicity of logging while not really solving any relevant problems. However, in practical terms, administrators can still accomplish what's needed through workarounds or by integrating the limited *systemd* toolset.

Before this chapter turns into a treatise against *systemd* or allowing people to solve problems that don't exist, the focus for a DevSecOps practitioner should be aimed toward enabling visibility and transparency throughout the software development lifecycle. That focus moves the discussion toward overall reliability of an application. A role within a DevSecOps organization that has touchpoints in all three areas is the site reliability engineer.

Site Reliability Engineering

Visibility and transparency are the goals for the site reliability engineer (SRE), and monitoring and logging/log analysis are the methods used to meet those goals. Other methods such as traceability of tests and code are also important. The problem is that visibility and transparency sometimes decrease performance or the efficient use of resources. For example, logging significant detail about every request on a moderately busy application reduces performance because compute and memory resources need to be allocated for the logging. At the same time, cost is increased not only because of the need for additional compute and memory but also because of the costs associated with storing the captured data.

Varying levels of information have to be captured without needing to restart or reinitialize services. This can be accomplished through feature flags that are examined while the system is running—for example, a feature flag that is queried on every request and enables more information to be logged about that request. Feature flags also become prominent around release and deployment of new versions of an application. A feature flag can enable a new feature after the code has been deployed through the continuous integration/continuous deployment (CI/CD) pipeline.

Table 3-2 earlier in this chapter contained criteria to help facilitate a choice around monitoring software. Ideal monitoring software can be deployed in such a way that new clients are added to and removed from the monitoring infrastructure automatically at time of deployment or decommissioning. From the perspective of an SRE, it will be practically impossible to add and remove individual hosts in a scaled DevSec-Ops organization. Therefore, the metrics to be monitored and how those metrics are monitored come into focus. Software like Ansible can add the new resource to the monitored device configuration automatically.

The level of detail to be monitored will vary. For example, whether there are two or two hundred compute resources responding to microservice API calls is irrelevant as long as the response time criteria are met. Further, the resources are deployed and decommissioned so rapidly that it may not make sense to monitor individual nodes or specific pieces of individual nodes such as disk allocation or used space on each node.

The answer to the timeless question "How much monitoring should we have?" is typically "As much as we can get." In reality, the answer will depend on the service, its use, and the longevity of each node. However, gathering more metrics and storing them is generally better than having fewer metrics, all things being equal.

Using disk input/output (I/O) as an example, if you are gathering I/O on each node and notice that suddenly with the latest software release you now need to deploy more nodes to service the same number of requests, it will be helpful to look back historically and see that I/O was much lower a week ago or a year ago or whatever timeframe.

The ability to drill down into increasingly granular data is a feature that some monitoring packages have. That feature wasn't included in Table 3-2 because the preference should be on security, ease of deployment, and flexibility around the primary mission of monitoring rather than reporting. All of the pretty graphs in the world aren't worth much if the client agent software caused a successful security attack to occur, something that has happened with agent-based monitoring software.

Many organizations will have a separate internal team that investigates security-related incidents. From the perspective of DevSecOps, observability and metrics captured through the standard DevSecOps practices help immensely in both discovery of incidents and then analysis and ultimately recovery from a security incident. Preservation of both environment and logged data are key elements of success for incident response and recovery.

Code Traceability and Static Analysis

Though deeper coverage of software testing appears in Chapter 4, I've included code traceability here because of its importance to security. Like many terms in computing, code traceability is overloaded, with different meanings in different contexts. For example, you might hear of code traceability in terms of tracing a line of code backward through the source code management history to the original change request that caused the developer to write it. You might also hear of code traceability referring to a developer or quality assurance tester being able to step through the code line by line, watching in-memory data as it changes. Other meanings also exist for code traceability.

For the purposes of this section, "code traceability" refers to the DevSecOps practitioner being able to step through the code to validate and verify its operation. Doing so may require the use of build-time flags to add more debugging instrumentation and logging. Consider an example of a microservice that is slow to respond. The person tasked with investigating the issue can "turn up" logging such that performance-based timings are recorded at key intervals within the code, such as an interaction with a data store. Now the investigator can see that the data store is slow to respond and take action accordingly.

Static analysis and code review

At a high level, "static analysis" refers to testing of software execution paths to identify problems within the code. From the perspective of DevSecOps, static analysis is part of a code review process where adherence to the coding style of an organization along with analysis for software errors and security vulnerabilities is measured. There are three primary types of issues that you can find through static analysis and code review:

- Errors and unexpected behavior (bugs)
- Security vulnerabilities that aren't error-like behaviors
- Code maintainability problems

An error can be found through testing of the code, using both positive and negative tests, both of which are discussed in Chapter 4. Whereas with testing, code is typically not used, with static analysis, the code is available to be examined. You may hear of this as "white box" testing, where the tester can see the code and other material. Having access to the code enables the tester to target specific areas where problems may occur. Merely getting the application to do something unexpected is evidence of an error that should be handled programmatically.

Causing the application to behave in an unexpected manner, allowing escalation of privilege, and improper data validation are examples of potential security vulnerabilities that can be found with static analysis. From the perspective of the developer, the code may work perfectly fine. Users can authenticate or an order is entered successfully. Only on closer inspection will you find that users don't need to be authenticated in order to view account details or view the shopping cart of another user.

Code maintainability is analyzed during code review and somewhat overlaps with the coding style of an organization. For example, a ternary is one method for implementing a condition (if-else) set in many languages. However, some organizations choose to avoid ternaries as they cause confusion for developers when compared to the more expressive syntax. As it pertains to analysis, then, an automated tool can be configured to flag ternaries as potentially difficult to maintain, while other organizations may not use that rule. Sometimes these types of issues are referred to as "code smells," though the term seems inexact, at best.

There are various tools to help with static analysis, and the DevSecOps workflow can be integrated such that static analysis is performed at the time of code check-in, or when the developer commits and pushes their code to a shared repository through the source code management (SCM) tool.

Compliance and regulatory issues

Static analysis and vulnerability scanning have become a normal part of the regular routine for a security analyst. These scans help to identify potential issues within the organizational infrastructure that may have come up through deployment of new software or through software updates. The scans can only go so far, and organizations may work only to the level of minimal compliance with necessary regulations, the letter of the law instead of the spirit of the law.

False positives are issues flagged by an automated scanner or other tool that aren't really issues at all. For example, a vulnerability scan noting an open port when that port is necessary for the underlying business application to function is an example of a false positive. Yes, an open port is technically an opportunity for an attacker to exploit a vulnerability. However, closing the port means that the business can no longer accept orders. Therefore, the issue isn't really relevant.

False positives waste time and resources because each will need to be documented so that a compliance officer will be happy. In the meantime, the tool did not notice several other issues that are truly going to cause problems and lead to successful attacks. When missed, these are called false negatives. The issues should have been noticed but were not. Finding false negatives currently takes some amount of expertise and human intervention. However, artificial intelligence will be able to replace much of this expertise in the coming years.

Becoming Security Aware

Years of industry experience combined with teaching programming courses for several years leads me to the conclusion that computer security problems frequently, though not always, can be traced back to two reasons. The first is lack of awareness on the part of the developer. For example, the developer was unaware that reflecting form data back to the user was a security problem.

The second reason for security problems is urgency imposed by often-artificial deadlines. I was part of a project that had been delayed for months and then years due to technical difficulties. The deadline for the project to be launched kept getting delayed and pushed further and further out. Somewhere within there, more than a year in advance, I booked a weeks-long trip to Europe. The trip was approved as official vacation time by the company and was nowhere near the deadline for the major project launch. You can probably guess where this is going. Sure enough, the project launch date was moved and overlapped with the vacation time. There was nothing special about the launch date. The date wasn't tied to any regulatory or compliance need or to a client or anything else and had been moved enough times that another move of a couple weeks wouldn't cause any difference. But the story has a happy ending. The launch date was moved yet again and didn't overlap, and the project eventually went live.

As alluded to, sometimes true deadlines do exist. Legal and regulatory compliance dates prevent proper security from being implemented. More often than not, it's simply trying to meet an artificial deadline. This book cannot hope to address the latter reason because the people who need to understand the effect of artificial deadlines won't read it anyway.

Finding Formal Training

Security training comes in many forms, from on-site to virtual, from classroom to hands-on. There will be no single class, video series, or book that could possibly ingrain all of the knowledge and put it in context of everyday use for a developer. Solving the problem of developers not being security aware should be individualized, based on their needs and prior experience. Ideally, this includes training that is customized for the organization and specific to the programming languages and infrastructure being used. However, barring a custom solution, a generalized training approach can be used.

Both SANS and ISC2 are well-known organizations that offer cybersecurity training. Both also have certification programs. In the case of ISC2, the Certified Information Systems Security Professional (CISSP) has been the gold standard for security certifications for a long time. The CISSP is aimed toward those with the word "Security" in their job title, but other certifications exist from both organizations. Even if certification isn't the goal, both organizations offer introductory training and learning paths that would be directly helpful for DevSecOps practitioners.

Obtaining Free Knowledge

The previous chapter alluded to the OWASP Top 10 as a resource for DevSecOps to learn about the types of attacks that are successful and how to mitigate those attacks. For example, the 2021 OWASP Top 10 list (*https://owasp.org/www-project-top-ten*) has Broken Access Control as the top item. Essentially everything identified within the realm of broken access control is within the purview of a DevSecOps team. The primary exception would be when integrating with third-party software or when using external/outsourced portions of a web application. There is limited recourse when good vendors go bad.

The number one access control vulnerability identified by OWASP is violating the concept of least privilege. Other issues include lack of authentication controls around API access, the ability for a user to escalate privilege or act as an administrator by changing the URL, and related issues. As a developer, preventing these types of vulnerabilities should be part of the development process.

Increasing awareness of the best practices for security during development is a convenient but far too cliché phrase. No one has ever said, "I'd like to decrease awareness of security" or "I'd like to increase awareness of worst practices for security." However, the contrast is the key detail: if there are *best practices* for security, then there must be *worst practices* or less-than-best, at least. That realization leads to interesting comparisons.

Developers who integrate security into the development process assume that all input is broken and that all external data is incorrect and may have been entered with malicious intent. This assumption then leads directly to validating all input against their version of the truth or the business rules for what is and is not valid data. For example, if a legacy system limits city names to 15 characters, then it is imperative to ensure that city names longer than 15 characters cannot be entered. A user may be entering a long city name to try to get the application to act in unknown or unhandled ways, or they could just live in Wisconsin Rapids, but it's up to the developer to assume that the city name will be longer and then truncate the city name or display an error, depending on the needs of the application.

Going beyond invalid data, what if the data doesn't exist at all? If it's a simple web application, HTML attributes and JavaScript provide client-side validation, but only if the end user has those enabled. The developer must always validate on the server side, meaning once the data has been submitted. In the case of an API, the developer must assume that the caller of the API has not sent in all data. When consuming data from an API, the developer must assume that not all fields were returned. Any and all data from external sources should be validated for existence and appropriateness.

The Common Vulnerabilities and Exposures (CVE) website (*https://cve.org*) is an authoritative source for vulnerabilities as they are announced. This site should be required reading or at least required skimming on a daily basis for DevSecOps practitioners.

Enlightenment Through Log Analysis

If you have the opportunity to get access to logfiles from a server operating on the internet, these can be valuable for learning about vulnerabilities and also how frequently servers are under attack. Granted, most of the attacks are fly-by attacks that are automated and looking for open ports or common issues. These "bot" attacks are usually merely annoyances, assuming that the system is up to date and has followed best practices for security.

We examine logfiles in some of the courses that I teach, specifically web server logfiles, email logs, and general access logs. Students are often surprised that bot attacks occur as often and with as much sophistication as is shown in the logfiles. For example, the web server access log shows thousands of lines of scans looking for vulnerable software and sometimes attempting to exploit that software. Examining the logfile helps students to understand why it's important to change settings away from their defaults when possible. If an automated scan finds an administrative account with the default password, it will be exploited.

At minimum, examining logfiles should prove enlightening to the types of vulnerabilities that are being sought, which should help avoid some of those common issues. Another potential benefit is finding an actual problem that attackers are exploiting on the system and then being able to stop the attack. A side effect of logfile analysis may also be an appreciation for the jobs done by server administrators!

Practical Implementation: OWASP ZAP

The term "DevSecOps" was originally just "DevOps," bringing development and operations closer to one another. A primary problem being solved with DevOps was the "throw it over the wall and forget about it" mentality that frequently occurred after a project was launched. Developers would test their code and launch it to production only to find that there were problems operating the software in the production environment. DevOps has helped to solve that problem by shifting operational needs left, or earlier in the development lifecycle.

Without the "Sec" in DevSecOps, the same problem could still occur. Security and compliance issues were not discovered until very late in the development lifecycle. Severe security problems would prevent the software from being released, thus causing confusion and delay. Even worse, security problems that went unnoticed would then lead to successful attacks against that software. Therefore, we've arrived at DevSecOps to integrate security earlier and throughout the development lifecycle.

As alluded to in the previous section, becoming security aware is a challenge of both knowledge and timeline, where developers may not know what they don't know and stakeholders may arrive at unrealistic deadlines, both of which are direct causes of security issues. Gaining knowledge takes experience, which is only earned by investing time and effort, and sometimes by being directly involved in a security-related issue. Gaining knowledge is generally under your own control because so many resources are free. However, the challenge of timeline is not as easily overcome. No solution has been discovered that will prevent a vice president of the company from overcommitting on a project. Therefore, tools have been created to help reduce the burden related to security validation.

OWASP Zed Attack Proxy (ZAP) is cross-platform software used for vulnerability scanning of web applications. ZAP provides a graphical interface and trivially easy method for DevSecOps organizations to scan for common problems highlighted on the OWASP website. Installing the graphical version of ZAP is a good starting place, but a word of caution: by default, even a scan by ZAP can be interpreted as an attack. Don't use ZAP if you're not authorized to scan a site, including internally. As an organization matures along the DevSecOps implementation, automation of ZAP scans should become part of the CI/CD pipeline.

Creating a Target

I own a chainsaw that came with an actual printed manual. The beginning of that manual is dedicated to the safety warnings commensurate with such a tool. I received the chainsaw as a gift, and after reading the manual and adhering to the proper safety protocol, I wanted to use that chainsaw to cut something. Not finding fallen trees on my own property, I decided to cut down a tree that was still standing, although generally unhealthy and leaning heavily. In retrospect, it was only sheer luck that made the tree fall in nearly the right place and without kicking back toward me. No amount of safety warnings make gravity disappear.

Just like a chainsaw, the tool I'm introducing in this section can be used incorrectly and with unintended consequences. Even though there are safety mechanisms in place to prevent problems, it is possible to remove those safeties and do actual damage to servers maintained by others. When using OWASP ZAP, you will load websites and potentially break them. Knowing that possibility exists, OWASP created "Juice Shop."

Juice Shop from OWASP is a demo web application that runs on a variety of platforms, including Node.js, Docker, and Vagrant, or as an instance on Amazon Web Services (AWS) Elastic Compute Cloud (EC2), Azure, or Google Compute Engine. The examples in this section will point toward an instance of the Juice Shop that I have running locally. Figure 3-5 shows the Juice Shop site, which even has a cookie notice!

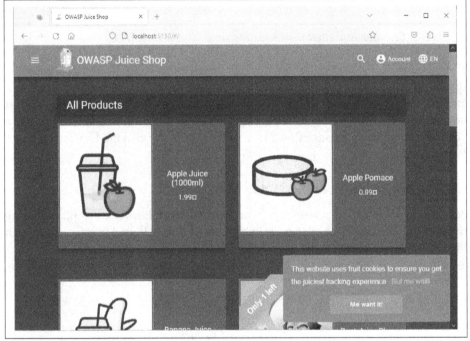

Figure 3-5. The OWASP Juice Shop site that can be used as a target for the ZAP tool

Go to OWASP Juice Shop (*https://owasp.org/www-project-juice-shop*) to find out more information, including how to download and install the Juice Shop site. The next section will examine some of the functionality of ZAP.

Installing ZAP

Installation of ZAP will depend on the platform that you're using: Linux, macOS, or Windows. See the ZAP download packages along with the installation instructions on the ZAP website (*https://www.zaproxy.org/download*). Once you've started ZAP, you will be prompted for how to handle persistence, meaning whether you want to be able to pick up where you left off at a later date. Figure 3-6 shows the prompt.

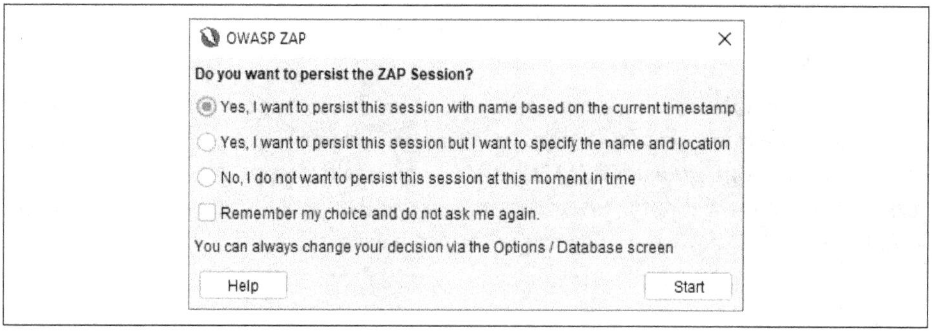

Figure 3-6. *Persistence prompt when starting ZAP*

If you're unsure, then selecting "Yes, I want to persist this session with name based on the current timestamp" is a safe option. You can also check the "Remember my choice and do not ask me again" checkbox if you'd like, though doing so is not required. If you select "No, I do not want to persist this session at this moment in time," then you can always change your mind and save the session by clicking File and selecting Persist Session later.

Getting Started with ZAP: Manual Scan

At a basic level, scanning a website for common vulnerabilities is accomplished using the Automated Scan button from the main area of the ZAP user interface, shown in Figure 3-7.

Figure 3-7. *The main user interface within ZAP*

However, when you do so, the option to enter a URL may be grayed out, as shown in Figure 3-8.

| URL to attack: | Attacking arbitrary URLs is not permitted in Protected or Safe mode. | ∨ | ● Select... |

Figure 3-8. The URL to attack text box is grayed out due to the ZAP mode

ZAP modes

ZAP operates in one of four modes, which provide some protection against inadvertently pointing ZAP toward a site that you do not own or performing another action that may be detrimental to one of your production web applications. Table 3-3 describes the four modes of operation for ZAP.

Table 3-3. Modes of operation for ZAP

Mode	Description
Safe Mode	Items considered dangerous are not allowed.
Protected Mode	Limited ability to scan unverified URLs.
Standard Mode	All actions are allowed.
ATTACK Mode	All actions are allowed, and when scanning, newly discovered items are also scanned.

As you may have gathered from the names of the four modes, ATTACK Mode could be viewed as an attack and can have ramifications beyond the URL to which the software was originally pointed. I'd recommend not using ATTACK Mode unless you've already gained significant experience with the inner workings of the software through the other modes. For now, if ZAP is not in Safe Mode, set it to Safe Mode by clicking the drop-down in the upper left of the ZAP toolbar, depicted in Figure 3-9. The mode can also be changed by clicking Mode from within the Edit menu.

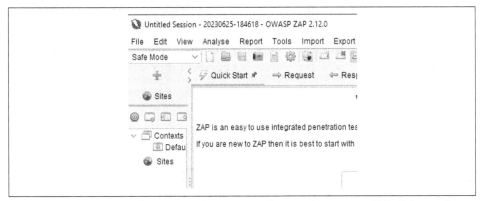

Figure 3-9. The upper-left corner of the ZAP window is where you will find the Mode drop-down

Safe Mode does not allow for automated scans, but you can manually explore a site this way. Click on Manual Explore from within the Quick Start tab of ZAP. When you do, you'll be presented with the Manual Explore screen. You can then point ZAP at the site of your choice. In the case of Figure 3-10, I am pointing at *http://localhost:5150*, which corresponds to the instance of the Juice Shop site that I am running.

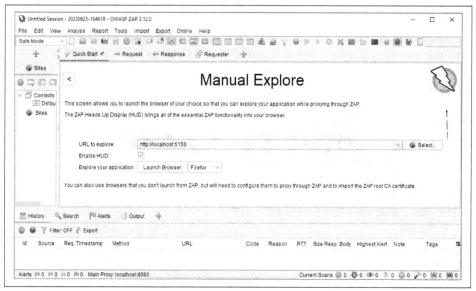

Figure 3-10. Manually exploring a site with ZAP

Other options available within the Manual Explore dialog are whether to enable the Heads Up Display (HUD) and which browser to launch. These options have been left at their default in Figure 3-10. Clicking Launch Browser starts Firefox through the proxy of ZAP.

As is evident in Figure 3-11, the ZAP HUD launches with an overlay that gives you two choices: "Take the HUD Tutorial" or "Continue to your target."

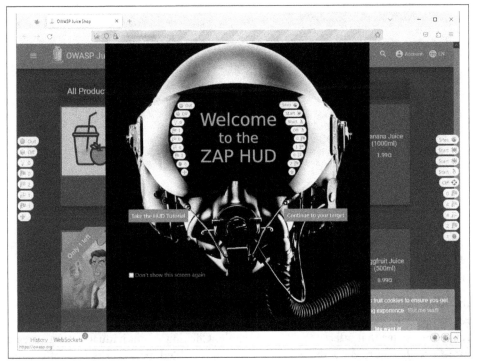

Figure 3-11. The ZAP HUD intro screen

I recommend taking the HUD Tutorial, which will help navigate the features of the HUD, but for now, click "Continue to your target." Like the HUD, the Juice Shop site will also present an overlay with informative information and options, shown in Figure 3-12.

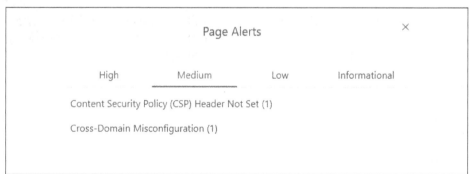

Figure 3-12. The Welcome overlay when running the Juice Shop site

Click Dismiss on the overlay and you'll see the Juice Shop site along with buttons on the left and right, which are part of the ZAP HUD. The buttons on the left side are related to issues found on this particular page, while the buttons on the right side are related to issues that affect the site as a whole. Clicking an individual button reveals more detail. Figure 3-13 shows alerts classified as Medium severity that affect the page.

	Page Alerts		✕
High	Medium	Low	Informational

Content Security Policy (CSP) Header Not Set (1)

Cross-Domain Misconfiguration (1)

Figure 3-13. Medium-severity issues that affect this particular page, as shown through the ZAP HUD

You can drill down to more information about the specific alert by clicking on one of the alerts from Figure 3-13. For example, Figure 3-14 shows additional detail about Cross-Domain Misconfiguration. Scrolling within that dialog box reveals additional information and a suggested solution.

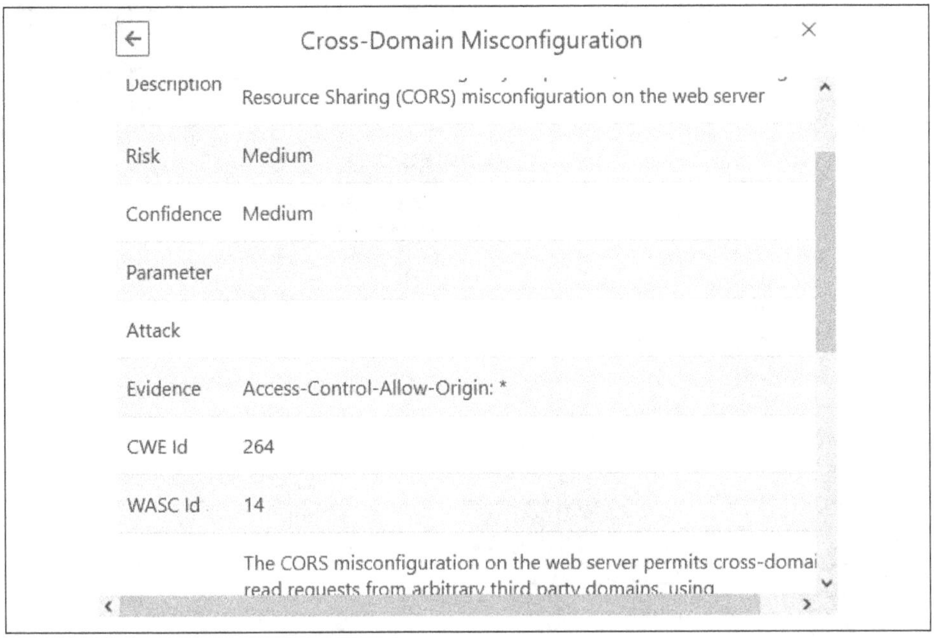

Cross-Domain Misconfiguration	
Description	Resource Sharing (CORS) misconfiguration on the web server
Risk	Medium
Confidence	Medium
Parameter	
Attack	
Evidence	Access-Control-Allow-Origin: *
CWE Id	264
WASC Id	14
	The CORS misconfiguration on the web server permits cross-domai read requests from arbitrary third party domains, using

Figure 3-14. Additional detail about an issue found with ZAP

Exploring a site manually is a good way to learn about ZAP while in the relatively safe confines of clicking through and interacting with the site as you normally might. However, doing so repeatedly as part of development and testing becomes both time-consuming and mind-numbing. Therefore, a more automated method is needed.

Using an automated scan

This section shows how to perform an automated scan against the local Juice Shop site with ZAP. I would not run this scan on a site that I didn't own or one that was hosted on a server that I didn't own, and I recommend against doing so. The first thing to do is change to Standard Mode by selecting it from the drop-down in the toolbar.

With Standard Mode enabled, click Automated Scan and enter the URL. Figure 3-15 shows the Automated Scan window with the URL for my local instance of the Juice Shop site.

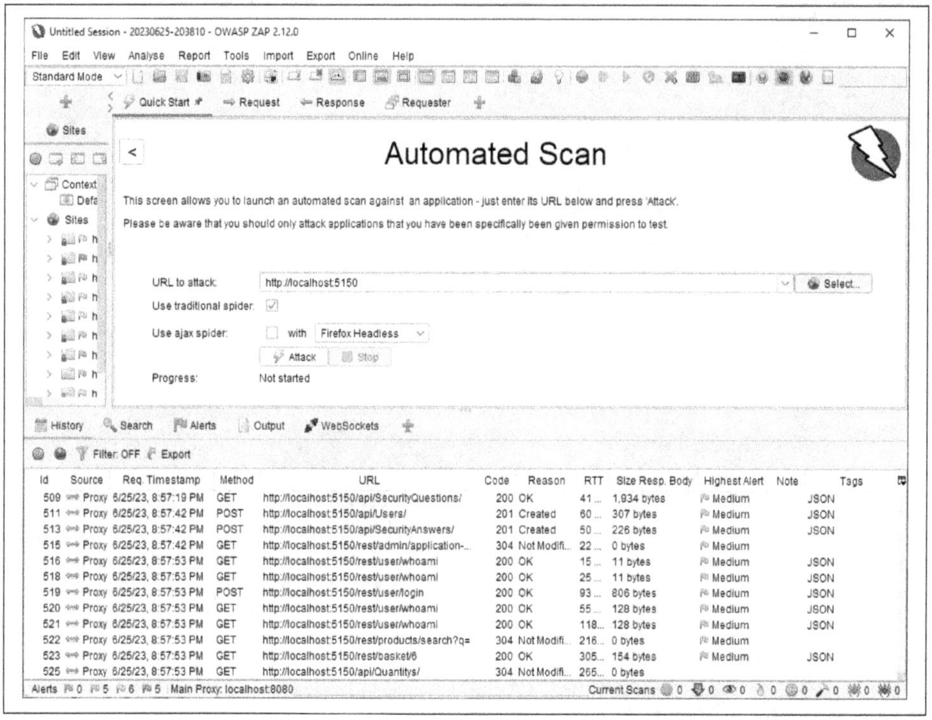

Figure 3-15. Starting an automated scan against a local copy of the Juice Shop site

Clicking Attack begins the process of an automated scan. When the scan begins, you may notice confetti appearing within the Juice Shop page. The confetti and subsequent alerts on the Juice Shop site indicate that you have solved some of the challenges that are included in the Juice Shop code. Figure 3-16 shows four such successes, including provoking an error that wasn't handled well by the site, accessing a confidential document, viewing someone else's shopping cart, and repeating registrations.

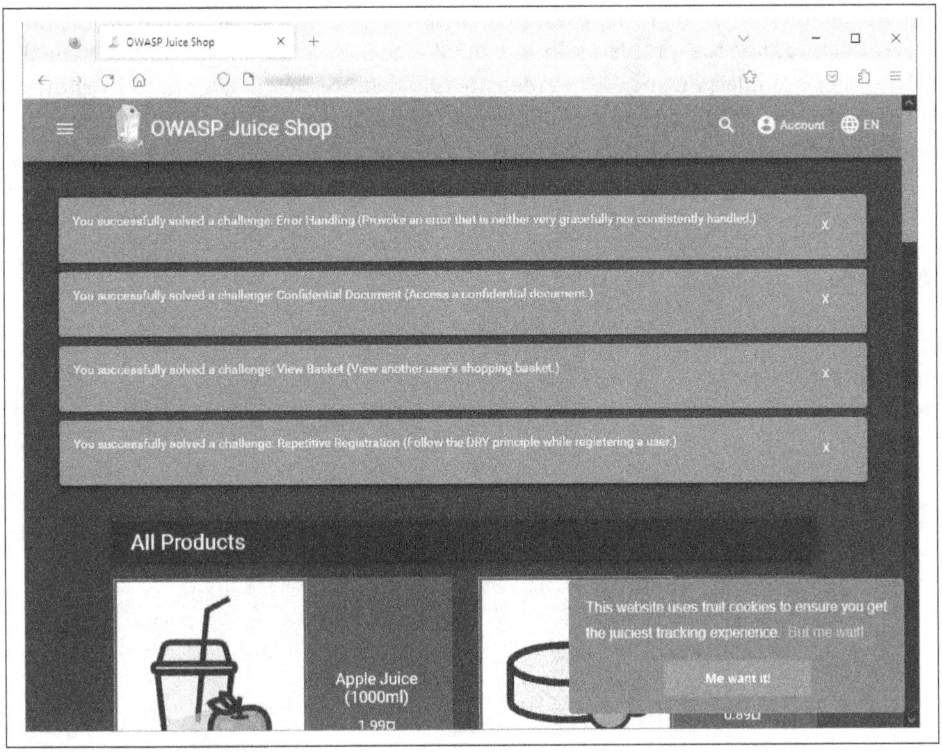

Figure 3-16. Successfully breaking the Juice Shop site with a ZAP automated scan

The ZAP automated scan will continue for quite some time against the Juice Shop site, with thousands of requests as the spider crawls through each page and discovers new resources, which then lead to more pages, which then leads to more resources. If you'd like to stop the scan for any reason, such as maybe pointing the tool toward a live site, you can do so by clicking the square that is found toward the bottom section of the ZAP interface, as shown in Figure 3-17.

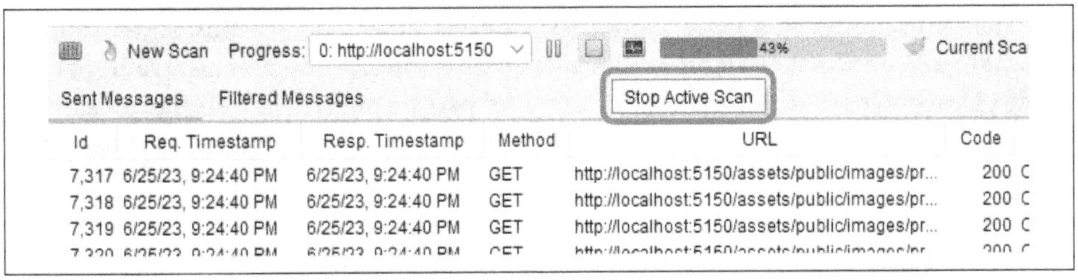

Figure 3-17. Stop the active scan by clicking the square toward the bottom half of the ZAP interface

When complete or when stopped, ZAP displays the Alerts tab, containing more information about the problems found on the site. Like the alerts shown with the HUD interface, alerts can be expanded to reveal more detail. Figure 3-18 shows a severe problem of SQL injection. In addition to information about the issue itself, this also shows the page and/or data that triggered the alert.

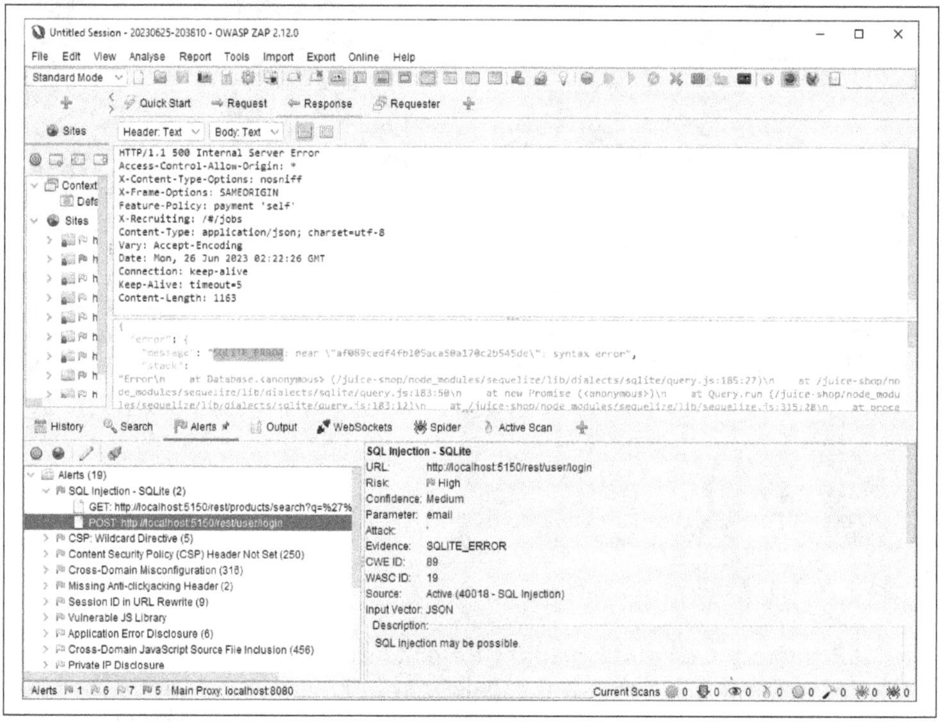

Figure 3-18. The results of a scan with additional information about the problem itself

The two scans, manual and automated, are some of the most basic usages of ZAP. The next phase of ZAP implementation would be to customize it for your web application and site while in development. Doing so is beyond the scope of this book, though. Another path—or further along on the same path—toward implementing automation within DevSecOps is to integrate ZAP scans as part of the testing process, as early as possible in that testing. ZAP can be executed from the command line and thus can be integrated into the CI/CD pipeline.

Summary

Much of computer security is merely theater, where a facade of security is all that people care about—right up until their business is attacked. It's not as though anyone in HR would know the difference, but computer security is not achieved by bullying employees into taking phishing training. Things like multifactor authentication provide proof that the attackers have already won. Rather than monitoring for and reacting to targeted attacks and attempts to compromise passwords, making everyone carry another form of verification only increases the attack footprint.

The focus of this chapter was on security, with the goal of integrating security throughout DevOps to create DevSecOps. The chapter expanded on the CIA triad with examples of each of the three and ended with a demonstration of the OWASP ZAP tool. The next chapter looks at development, with coverage intended to show tools and processes for delivering successful software.

## CHAPTER 4

Managing Code and Testing

Three stages within the DevSecOps lifecycle focus on traditionally developer-related tasks. These include the development or coding itself, building the resulting code into an executable application, and testing the application. Full testing would involve other teams such as quality assurance (QA), but at least some tests are done at the developer level. The build step is significantly customized depending on the programming language in use. Some languages require compiling of artifacts, while others can be deployed in an uncompiled state. The chapter begins with a focus on development and wraps up with concepts and tools for testing software. Along the way, the chapter also introduces Git for source code management and two patterns for using Git when developing software.

Examining Development

With the number of programming languages available, it is impossible to provide a single section, a single chapter, or maybe even a single book that distills all of the knowledge needed to be a successful developer in that language. There are also numerous books covering high-level programming design and architectural concerns as well. Though it will seem self-serving, a general rule that I've followed in my career is to look for books published by O'Reilly, because the books have thorough coverage. In the area of software design and architecture, Martin Fowler has written several books that are canonical in their respective areas in the same way that the *TCP/IP Illustrated* series by W. Richard Stevens was the go-to source for many years. With respect given to those and other related works, there are a few ideas that I try to relate to my students working on production-style programming. Also noteworthy is that these ideas are themselves distillations of the ideas of the aforementioned and others, but I have found them eminently helpful and approachable for students.

Be Intentional and Deliberate

Even before artificial intelligence enabled people to receive viable-looking answers to coding problems, developers were borrowing code from others. Whether the code worked exactly correctly or fit the design was sometimes a distant second place to simply completing the task. This is where being intentional and deliberate are relevant. A developer could technically complete the task with nested loops and hardcoded values, but doing so would introduce technical debt and may not work correctly beyond the narrow focus of the current task and with limited testing. Consider this code that assumes there will always be 50 states in the United States and that their alphabetical order will always remain the same:

```
for (i = 0; i < 50; i++):
  if (i == 49):
    state_name = "Wisconsin"
```

While the example may be somewhat extreme, this type of hardcoding exists when there are time pressures or other factors that cause a developer to consider the code to be complete when it may not be fully developed.

 "Technical debt" is a term used to describe borrowing time from future development or advancement of an application or system. Hardcoding values in a program rather than abstracting the values to a variable or constant may save time for this one single task with a single value of test data, but the next time that value is needed, it will have to be hardcoded again. If the value ever changes in the future, then all of those locations where the value was hardcoded will need to be changed, potentially introducing errors. While the time was saved for the single instance in the one file, that time will be repaid later, just as a monetary debt would be repaid at a later date.

Don't Repeat Yourself

Consider this code that is used to calculate the total for an order by multiplying the subtotal by the tax rate (5.5%):

```
order_tax = subtotal * 0.055
```

If the tax rate never changes and does not need to be used anywhere else in the application, this code meets the criteria for a minimally viable product (MVP). However, another developer is also working on a portion of the application that needs the tax rate. Instead of using the decimal representation of the tax percentage, they choose to use the percentage itself. Their code looks like this:

```
order_tax = subtotal * 5.5
```

These two pieces of code will produce wildly different values. The developer may not notice the problem because the math is technically correct, as in the value produced by the multiplication operator produces a correct result.

Instead of relying on hardcoded values, a constant could be used for the tax rate:

```
const TAX_RATE = 0.055
order_tax = subtotal * TAX_RATE
```

There is less confusion with the use of a constant. In addition to less confusion, there is now only one place to change the tax rate when the rate increases in the future.

Managing Source Code with Git

Whether developing as part of a team or as a soloist, tracking changes to source code enables you to look back at the history of changes to the code. You can then revert back to an old version of the code should something break with a newly introduced code. Source code management (SCM) tools such as CVS, SVN, Mercurial, Git, and others provide the ability to track changes.

In an organizational setting, there's a good chance that code from different parts of a project is shared and worked on by multiple developers simultaneously. Each developer makes changes, which are tracked by the SCM. When the code is uploaded to a common SCM server, the changes from each developer are merged with one another, producing a single coherent set of software files containing all of the changes from those developers. Linus Torvalds, creator of the Linux kernel, created the Git SCM tool. Git is a popular open source SCM that is widely used. This section looks at two methods for managing source code with Git: the Gitflow pattern and the trunk-based pattern. But first, we'll establish a baseline or minimal pattern.

A Simple Setup for Git

This section outlines a method for using Git on a private and independent server, such as a server housed on premises in an organization. The obvious advantages include privacy and cost. There would be no need for hosting the source code repository at a third party, and there is no cost for Git regardless of the number of developers who use it within an organization. The disadvantage is a slightly more difficult integration, depending on the number of users who need access.

This section assumes that you have a Linux server running and have installed Git and an SSH server. If you have not, then a Linux instance can be deployed on AWS or another cloud provider. Both Git and an SSH server are available through the package management tools of most major Linux distributions.

Referring to a Git server is somewhat of a misnomer. A Git server does not run any special software other than the same Git-related commands that run on a client. The "server" is merely an agreement that you will use a central location from which source code will be uploaded and downloaded. For many, that central location is GitHub, but for others, it's an internal server.

One of the protocols that you can use for communication between client and "server" with Git is SSH. Because SSH is a key technology behind many other DevSecOps processes, using SSH for Git also makes sense because the software has typically been installed for other reasons.

The Git usage patterns in this section both rely on role-based access control through groups. In other words, users are added to the Linux server, and those users are then added to groups. For example, a group called *gitusers* is created. Members of that group have access to the Git repositories. The following example demonstrates sharing of a repository by two users. The assumption is that the users already exist. Afterward, the users will both be able to commit to and fetch changes from the other user. The two usernames are *suehring* and *rkonkol* for the example, and they will both be added to the *gitusers* group. The repository in the example is named *devsecops* and is stored in the */opt/git/* directory on the server. More complex scenarios are available for sharing, whether with Git or with other software such as GitHub.

Add a user called *gituser*:

```
adduser gituser
```

Change the shell of the *gituser* account. When prompted, change the shell to */usr/bin/git-shell*:

```
chsh gituser
```

Create a *.ssh* directory within the home directory of *gituser*:

```
cd /home/gituser && mkdir .ssh
```

Change ownership of the *.ssh* directory as well as its permissions:

```
chown gituser.gituser .ssh && chmod 700 .ssh
```

Add an *authorized_keys* file within the *.ssh* directory and change its permissions. Technically this step isn't required right now but will save a step later:

```
touch .ssh/authorized_keys
chmod 600 .ssh/authorized_keys
```

Add a group called *gitusers*:

```
groupadd gitusers
```

Add the two accounts for your developers:

```
adduser suehring
adduser rkonkol
```

Add each user to the *gitusers* group:

```
usermod -G gitusers suehring
usermod -G gitusers rkonkol
```

Have each of the developers generate SSH keys using the `ssh-keygen` command. You can also do this for the developers by becoming them, or assuming their identity, by using the `su` command, such as:

```
su - suehring
```

For completeness, if you are logged in as (or have assumed) the *suehring* user:

```
mkdir .ssh
chmod 700 .ssh
cd .ssh
ssh-keygen
```

accept the defaults for filename and determine whether you would like to add a passphrase to the key.

When an SSH key is generated, a pair of files will be created. By default the files are called *id_rsa* and *id_rsa.pub*. The *id_rsa* file is a private key, and the *id_rsa.pub* file is a public key. The private key should be kept private and not shared with anyone, while the public key can be shared.

To that end, copy the contents of the public key for each user to a file called *authorized_keys* within the *gituser* home directory. This step enables both of the developers to SSH as *gituser*. Be sure to use two greater-than signs for this command, otherwise the contents of *authorized_keys* will be overwritten.

Assuming that your current working directory contains the file *id_rsa.pub*, which it will if you followed the previous set of commands, run the following to add the key to the *authorized_keys* file for gituser. This command should be run for each of the developers using the contents of their individual public-key file:

```
cat id_rsa.pub >> ~gituser/.ssh/authorized_keys
```

The steps completed thus far are one-time foundational steps that need to be completed to prepare the server. In the future, only the developer accounts will be created and an SSH key generated and added to the *authorized_keys* file. It gets easier after the initial setup!

With these steps complete, it's time to create a Git repository. On the Git server, run this command to create the directory that will hold the repository:

```
mkdir /opt/git/devsecops.git && cd /opt/git/devsecops.git
```

As noted before, this server uses */opt/git* as the base for Git repositories. You might store the repositories elsewhere based on your organizational standard.

Create the repository:

```
git init --bare --shared=group
```

Change ownership and permissions:

```
chown -R gituser.gitusers /opt/git/devsecops.git
chmod 770 /opt/git/devsecops.git
```

That's it. The next time you need to add a repository, you can simply run the commands to initialize the repository and change its ownership and permissions, because the *gituser* account and the developer accounts were already created.

At this point, the developer should be able to clone the Git repository to their local development environment. This command assumes a server name of *source.example.com*. Change that according to your server naming convention:

```
git clone gituser@source.example.com:/opt/git/devsecops.git
```

If this is the first time that the developer has SSHed into the server, they will be prompted to accept the host key from the server. Assuming that the host key is valid and correct, typing "yes" will result in a clone of the Git repository being downloaded into a directory called *devsecops* in the current directory.

Now that the setup has been done, it's time to look at using Git.

Using Git (Briefly)

There are a handful of commands that you will use frequently with Git. The basic idea is:

1. Clone repository.
2. Write code.
3. Commit code.
4. Push code.

If you are working with other developers, then you'd add an additional step:

5. Merge code.

It is that final step, merge code, where all of life's problems occur and which is a major contributing factor for why DevSecOps is needed. More on merging later.

You've already seen two Git commands, `git init` and `git clone`. Initializing a repository is done once per repository, so the `git init` command will be used infrequently. Cloning a repository will occur more often, every time you need to download a new copy of the repository. However, once the repository is cloned, you will use other commands to interact with it to send your code to the server and to retrieve code from others in that same repository.

There is no Git-specific command for the step labeled "write code" that I mentioned earlier. However, after the code is written, those changes should be committed to the repository. There are two primary paths through which code is tracked within a repository:

- Adding a new file with new code
- Adding code to a file that already exists in the repository

When a new file is added within a Git repository, that file needs to be tracked so that changes are noted and a history of those changes is maintained. The `git add` command is used to add a new file to be tracked by a Git repository. This command adds a file called *README.md* to an existing repository:

```
git add README.md
```

From that point forward, changes to the file *README.md* will be tracked by Git within this repository.

When a file already exists within the repository, which is equivalent to saying, "Git knows about the file," then changes are tracked but need to be committed to the repository. Another way to think of a commit is as a checkpoint or a point-in-time snapshot of the contents of the file or files at that moment. An important conceptual difference between Git and other SCM tools is that the `git add` command will also be executed every time you want to commit changes to the file. This concept can be confusing and bears additional explanation.

Recall that a repository called *devsecops* was created in the previous section. That repository contains nothing; it is empty except for a *.git* directory that contains metadata managed by Git itself. When a file is added to the *devsecops* directory, the file is in an untracked state, meaning that Git is aware that the file exists within the *devsecops* directory but that the file will be ignored.

Untracked is one of two states in which files exist within a Git repository. Another state for a file within a repository is the *tracked* state. When files become known to Git within a repository, they are referred to as tracked. But those two states tell only part of the story. When a file becomes tracked, Git begins monitoring that file for changes. It's here that conceptual problems begin around the terms "state" versus "status." For practical purposes, untracked files are irrelevant to the repository, and therefore that's where we will leave them and focus instead on tracked files.

Is "Untracked" Really a Status Then?

The source code for Git contains this:

```
static const char *wt_status_diff_status_string(int status)
{
    switch (status) {
    case DIFF_STATUS_ADDED:
    return _("new file:");
    case DIFF_STATUS_COPIED:
    return _("copied:");
    case DIFF_STATUS_DELETED:
    return _("deleted:");
    case DIFF_STATUS_MODIFIED:
    return _("modified:");
    case DIFF_STATUS_RENAMED:
    return _("renamed:");
    case DIFF_STATUS_TYPE_CHANGED:
    return _("typechange:");
    case DIFF_STATUS_UNKNOWN:
    return _("unknown:");
    case DIFF_STATUS_UNMERGED:
    return _("unmerged:");
    default:
    return NULL;
    }
}
```

When a file is tracked, it will be forever tracked by Git. The file exists in one of these statuses:

- Unmodified
- Modified
- Staged

An unmodified file is one that has not changed since the last commit. With existing repositories that were just cloned, all files are unmodified because they were just downloaded from the remote repository. However, when a tracked file is changed, Git refers to the file as having a modified status.

Simply being modified does not mean that the file will be committed or able to be seen by other developers. To be committed and eventually seen by other developers, the file needs to be staged. A staged file is one that will be included in the next commit.

The difference between modified and staged is as fundamental as the difference between tracked and untracked. Having modified versus staged files enables you to choose which specific files to commit. You might also make multiple commits so that each commit creates its own snapshot with its own files. You might never need to separate commits in such a way, but the flexibility of having modified versus staged is available, should you ever need it.

Committing changes to the repository is accomplished with the `git commit` command. Assume that a file called *index.php* already exists in the repository.

If you make changes to the file, you still need to add the file to the staging for this commit using `git add`. After `git add` has been executed, the next step is to commit the staged changes:

```
git commit
```

The code itself is saved as a checkpoint and added to the history metadata tracked by Git. When you execute `git commit`, you are prompted to add a commit message. The commit message is a short message about the commit itself. For example, if you added a new title to *index.php*, then you might add the message "Added new title." This message is then viewable within the commit history of the repository (more on this later).

If you don't want to be prompted for a commit message and also don't want to execute `git add` for every change to a tracked file, you can add a couple of command-line options that alleviate the need for both. The following command is the equivalent of executing `git add` and `git commit` and then adding the previous message through a text editor:

```
git commit -a -m "Added new title"
```

The `-a` option adds files to the commit that have previously been added or made known to the repository. The `-m` option adds a message.

Even though the changes have been committed to the repository, those changes are only stored on your local machine. This means that the changes are not viewable by other developers and, importantly, are not being backed up in any way other than backups that you might have set up for your local development machine. The final step is to send the code back to the server. This is accomplished with the `git push` command, simply:

```
git push
```

Code is uploaded to the server from which the repository was first cloned.

 If you aren't sure where the code will be going, use the following command:

```
git remote show origin
```

Doing so will display the destination for the `git push` command.

You can view the commit history of the repository with the `git log` command. When you execute `git log`, the commits that are known within the repository are shown. It's worth noting that the commit history does not communicate with the server, so the history shown is limited to that which has been downloaded or cloned from the repository.

Branching and Merging

In an ideal world, a single developer is responsible for all of the code for an application. That developer never misunderstands a requirement, requirements are never missed, their code is perfect, and there are never bugs or other errors beyond their control.

In the real world, developers work in teams, requirements are missed and misinterpreted, bugs are introduced, and bugs are found that are outside of the control of the developers. When developers work in teams, the shared code can sometimes be a source of errors. If the developers implement a data structure differently or simply misspell a variable, errors occur when the code is merged. The later the merge occurs, the more impact the error will have on prior steps.

Restated, there is a greater chance of a bug impacting the release date when code is brought together and tested later. For example, fixing the bug means that previously tested code needs to be retested. If another part of the code relied on the bug or worked around the bug, then that other code may need to be rewritten.

Branching in SCM provides a means to work on code in parallel without affecting others. When a repository is cloned, the master or main branch is cloned. From this main branch, a developer may create a new branch to work on the code for a new feature. Simultaneously, other developers may be doing the same thing, each creating their own branch of the code, all separate from one another.

Creating a branch within a Git repository is accomplished with the `git branch` command. For example, if you wanted to create a branch called `project5` to work on changes related to the new website title, you use the following command:

```
git branch project5
```

The branch is then created, using the current code as its base. While the branch has been created, any changes that you make will remain within the current branch until you switch to the newly created branch. This is accomplished with the `git checkout` command, as in:

```
git checkout project5
```

Just like the options added onto the `git commit` command earlier, so too can you add a command-line option to the `git checkout` command that will create the branch and switch to it all at once:

```
git checkout -b project5
```
Changes to code and the commits related to those changes will now be sent to the `project5` branch. The `git merge` command is used when code needs to be brought back into the main branch. Merging examines each object in the repository to determine if there are changes to be included between the two branches of code. Git does its best to determine which object is the latest version and to resolve conflicts between two files that have changed between the branches. For more information, see the Basic Branching and Merging section (*https://git-scm.com/book/en/v2/Git-Branching-Basic-Branching-and-Merging*) within the official Git documentation, where you can find further details on merging and what can be done if a merge conflict occurs.

While branching keeps code from multiple developers logically separate, it does not solve the issue of late merges introducing bugs and untested behaviors. Multiple methods exist for managing team-based development. One such method is the Gitflow pattern, which we'll look at next.

Examining the Gitflow Pattern

Gitflow describes a process for sharing code through Git that uses separate development paths. Gitflow uses branching. Figure 4-1 shows the Gitflow pattern.

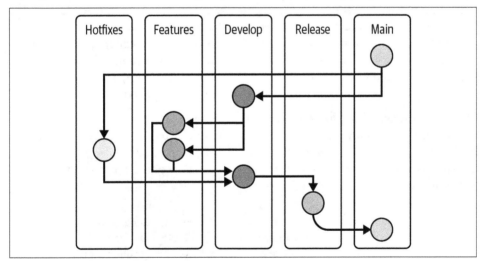

Figure 4-1. Typical Gitflow SCM pattern

As Figure 4-1 shows, there are several swimlanes within which active development takes place, while other swimlanes are reserved for the main line of production or released code. A walk-through of code through Gitflow helps to illustrate how changes are applied and then brought back into a release before being sent to production. Consider some code for a website. On Day 1 when the code is released, a bug is found. The bug needs to be fixed immediately. Therefore, a developer creates a branch to apply a hotfix. In Figure 4-1, the hotfix appears within the Hotfix swimlane. However, the developer finds that the bug is somewhat larger than anticipated and thus continues to determine how to fix it.

Meanwhile, development begins on enhancements to the site. This is reflected by a Develop swimlane and corresponding branch. The development branch is further split into feature branches so that multiple developers can work together on this development iteration or sprint. As features are completed, the code is merged back into the Develop branch. Eventually, the features and hotfixes (just one Hotfix in Figure 4-1) are merged with a Release branch.

The Release branch contains code that is ready to be deployed. Various elements are brought together at this final stage, though the exact components and processes vary from organization to organization and from release to release. For example, some organizations will have a formal build process, where code is compiled and final tests are executed. Other organizations may have a longer beta testing phase with a release candidate.

During the merge process between each swimlane in the Gitflow architecture, there can be one or more layers of approval prior to the merge being allowed. These gatekeeping processes serve as a checkpoint to ensure that unwanted code and side effects for that code are not introduced into the release or main branches or out to the production environment. A larger problem is that development branches tend to remain active for a long time. Features and hotfixes are merged into the development branch, but sometimes a hotfix isn't applied or is overwritten by later code that then reintroduces the issue for which the hotfix was originally applied.

With DevOps and then DevSecOps, an emphasis was placed on continuous integration/continuous deployment (CI/CD) and the automated testing that is necessary to deploy code to production with minimal checks. The premise is to move testing earlier and more often, essentially shifting the testing phase more to the left in a traditional waterfall SDLC model.

 When you read or hear "shift left," the shift is referring to moving testing and other elements of software development earlier so that problems are captured and addressed before being compounded.

With an emphasis on automation and de-emphasis of formal and manual approval processes, a new method for branching was developed. This new method is simplified from the Gitflow pattern, and that is the focus of the next section.

Examining the Trunk-Based Pattern

The premise behind the trunk-based pattern is to do away with long-lived development branches in favor of committing and frequently pushing code to a main branch, often called the trunk, so that the code can be tested and deployed. Figure 4-2 shows an example of the trunk-based pattern.

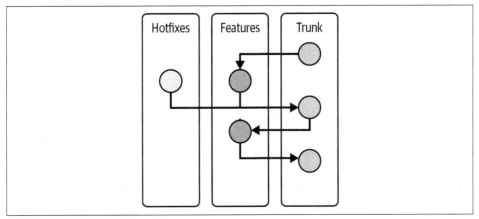

Figure 4-2. The trunk-based pattern for managing source code

Comparing the trunk-based pattern to the Gitflow pattern, you'll notice fewer swimlanes: just Trunk, Features, and Hotfixes. The idea is to promote from the Trunk, which is necessarily short-lived in order to avoid large merges. It's worth noting that both the Releases and Main branches can sometimes exist, but that's more so a logical or process-related necessity instead of a requirement for trunk-based development.

"Promote early, promote often" is the main idea for trunk-based development. That sounds great in theory, but in practice the implication is that a mature and thorough testing infrastructure exists and is capable of testing the application. This is the concept of *code coverage*. Code coverage describes the ratio of code to tests of that code. For example, consider this simple conditional statement:

```
if ($productType == "grocery") {
    $taxable = false;
}
```

A positive test for this code is to set the contents of the $productType variable to *grocery* and then examine whether $taxable is true, false, or unset afterward. Another test is to set $productType to anything other than the string of characters *grocery* and then examine the contents of the variable $taxable afterward. It would be tempting to indicate that the code coverage is 100% for this code. However, what if $productType is not set? The answer depends largely on the code that would be above the example shown here. Some languages will also not allow $productType to be unset and would provide an error during the compile process. Therefore, code coverage will depend on language and context.

The turn toward code coverage leads the chapter toward the concept of testing, which coincidentally is the next section. Choosing a branching strategy is not a permanent decision. I recommend trying (or continuing with) more formalized and deliberate patterns for code management to better understand where gaps exist in development, testing, and deployment. As you improve development practices, testing coverage, and deployment, simplify the code management processes to keep them from getting in the way of progress.

Testing Code

Examining an application for defects is accomplished at various stages throughout the SDLC. At the most basic level, a developer tests their own code. Consider the conditional statement from the previous section. A developer would likely test their code for the cases described in that section, testing both the positive case with the product type set to *grocery* and at least one negative case with the product type set to something other than *grocery*.

This section examines several aspects of testing, from basic developer tests to QA testing by end users. Included in the discussion of testing are both functional and nonfunctional requirements. Recall from Chapter 1 that a nonfunctional requirement is something like security or transaction speed. While it's possible that these are highlighted as specific requirements, it's more likely that requirements gathering will not include questions like "How fast would you like the application to load?" Instead, nonfunctional requirements may rely on service-level agreements.

Unit Testing

The conditional code shared earlier in this chapter would be part of a larger block of code that is tested by the developer as they write the code. When tested in small units, at the function level or similarly small pieces of code, this is called unit testing. There is no strict rule as to how small or how large a block of code can be and still be considered a unit test. However, as the number of dependencies increases, it becomes less likely that the test would be considered a unit test. Put another way, if the code being tested depends on several other files and preconditions, then the test is more akin to an integration test, where multiple elements are combined.

A basic goal of unit testing is 100% coverage of all conditions, such as the condition shared earlier. In addition, static analysis should be performed on the code. Static analysis describes a means to examine the code without executing it. Static analysis is frequently used for verifying adherence to coding standards and to validate basic application security.

Unit testing exists regardless of DevSecOps processes. However, moving toward DevSecOps means automating as many unit tests as possible. Ideally, all unit tests should be executed in an automated manner. Doing so facilitates the CI/CD processes needed to fully leverage DevSecOps.

Integration Testing

Integration testing brings together units of code to verify that those units work together to achieve the functional requirements of the application. Reaching the level of integration testing implies that unit tests are complete and successful. Where connections between units of code exist, integration testing verifies that those connections are working as intended.

System Testing

The third level of testing is commonly referred to as system testing. The goal with system testing is to combine all components in an environment that is as close to a production environment as possible. Both functional and nonfunctional tests should be performed in system testing, and ideally the data used will be a de-identified version of production data or a subset thereof. The caveat around whether a subset of data is acceptable is that using only a fraction of the data may hide performance-related problems. For example, if the normal production dataset is a multiterabyte legacy database and one of the features of the application requires querying that data, then using only a few gigabytes may mask a problem with the query. In the testing environment, the query may return results with acceptable performance, but when the entire dataset is queried, the results take minutes to return.

Automating Tests

Automation is a key factor in determining the success of any DevSecOps efforts. There are numerous tools available that help automate testing of code. One such tool is Selenium (*https://www.selenium.dev*). Selenium provides a full-featured test suite that can be scaled to distribute tests from multiple locations, and an IDE to help with creation of tests. There are also Python bindings for the underlying Selenium web driver.

Retrieving a page using Selenium and Firefox

You can execute Selenium tests from the command line using Python. Doing so enables you to build a simple means to test during development but also to create a sophisticated bot that can crawl the site as you create it, taking screenshots along the way to prove that a page exists and was rendered without error. This section shows Selenium with a headless Firefox browser running on Debian Linux. Later in the book, I'll show you a more complex example using Docker. The simple example shown in Example 4-1 seems to be missing from many of the tutorials that exist online. While the example lacks some of the debugging options and other niceties that you might want, such as a try/catch block, those can be added later.

Example 4-1. Basic Python code to retrieve a web page and capture the results

```
#!/usr/bin/env python

from selenium import webdriver

proto_scheme = "https://"
url = "www.braingia.org"

opts = webdriver.FirefoxOptions()
opts.add_argument('--headless')

driver = webdriver.Firefox(options=opts)
driver.implicitly_wait(10)

driver.get(proto_scheme + url)
driver.get_screenshot_as_file('screenshot.png')

result_file = 'page-source_' + url

with open(result_file,'w') as f:
  f.write(driver.page_source)
  f.close()
driver.close()
driver.quit()
```

Within Example 4-1, the first line interrogates the environment for a Python executable and enables execution of the file as a normal command rather than needing to preface the filename with "python" on the command line. For example, you'll see numerous examples online where programs written in Python are executed like this:

```
python3 program.py
```

Instead, by including the interpreter on the first line as shown, the file can be executed like this:

```
./program.py
```

The assumption is that the file is executable; if not, then you can chmod u+x program.py to add the executable bit.

Python 3 should be the default. If not, or if you receive errors regarding the version of Python in use on your system, you can remove this line completely and execute the file as shown earlier, by prefacing with the Python 3 interpreter.

The webdriver from Selenium is imported next, followed by two variables to establish both the protocol scheme and hostname to be tested. The next three lines set an option to execute Firefox in a headless manner. The headless option is used so that an X Window system or desktop environment does not need to be installed for this program to work. Firefox simply executes behind the scenes without need for the graphical interface.

The following line sets a wait time of 10 seconds. This can be adjusted as necessary for your environment. Ten seconds was chosen arbitrarily for this example. The web page is retrieved with the next line, and a screenshot is captured and named *screenshot.png*. The last section of the program opens a local file for writing and places the page source into that file. Finally, the session is closed and the browser quits executing.

It is worth noting that the program executes a copy of Firefox in the background. If the final call to quit() is not executed because of an earlier error, then there will be orphaned Firefox processes running on the system. A reboot of the computer would solve it, but because this is Linux, a reboot shouldn't be necessary. You can find the leftover Firefox processes with this command:

```
ps auwx | grep -i firefox
```

The resulting output will look something like this, although the username and process IDs will be different:

```
suehring 1982868 51.9 16.3 2868572 330216 pts/1  Sl
     12:12  25:43 firefox-esr --marionette --headless --remote
```

Issuing the kill command on the process ID will stop the process from running. In the example, the process ID is **1982868**. Therefore, the following command should be issued in order to stop this process:

```
kill 1982868
```

As noted earlier, an obvious improvement would be to include much of the processing within a try/catch block, which will alleviate some of the chance of orphaned processes being left over after an error. Another improvement would be to capture the initial URL as a command-line option along with the ability to crawl the site, collecting links found on the site and visiting those. Some may not consider those to be necessary or even an improvement. Therefore, simple is better, and this example shows the basics of retrieving a page.

Retrieving text with Selenium and Python

The previous example shows the use of Python, Selenium, and Firefox to retrieve the source from a web page and take a screenshot of that page. As part of testing, you may want to be alerted to a page not rendering correctly or with the correct elements or text within those elements. For example, if you've written tests to log in to a page and then expect a greeting on the next page that should contain your name, you can write a test to retrieve the specified HTML element and verify that the correct name is displayed within that element.

Text can be retrieved using a few methods. Example 4-2 shows a means to retrieve the copyright notice from a page if that notice is contained within a <p> element, as it is on my site currently.

Example 4-2. Retrieving a web page and displaying the copyright notice

```python
#!/usr/bin/env python

from selenium import webdriver

proto_scheme = "https://"

url = "www.braingia.org"
opts = webdriver.FirefoxOptions()
opts.add_argument('--headless')
driver = webdriver.Firefox(options=opts)

driver.implicitly_wait(10)
driver.get(proto_scheme + url)
driver.get_screenshot_as_file('screenshot.png')
copyright = driver.find_element("xpath", "//p[contains(text(),'Copyright')]")
print(copyright.text)
result_file = 'page-source_' + url
with open(result_file,'w') as f:
  f.write(driver.page_source)
  f.close()
driver.close()
driver.quit()
```

The two substantive changes are shown in bold within the listing for Example 4-2. You could also simply print the text on one line, like so:

```python
print(driver.find_element("xpath","//p[contains(text(),'Copyright')]").text)
```

However, I lean toward the version shown in Example 4-2 because that version enables manipulation of the element for uses other than showing the text.

Summary

This chapter provided information on development and testing. Being intentional and deliberate is understated among development paradigms and patterns. However, the phrase "intentional and deliberate" captures the essence behind knowing why you're using a pattern or even a line of code in a certain location. We also examined the Git SCM tool, along with the Gitflow and trunk-based architectures for managing code from creation through deployment. Finally, I discussed three levels of testing and provided test automation examples using Selenium and Python. My goal with the examples was to provide a simple baseline or foundation to which you can add additional complexity.

Chapter 5 continues to focus on DevSecOps practices with management of configuration as code. Developing with containerization techniques is frequently part of DevSecOps and modern development. Chapter 5 also demonstrates Docker.

Moving Toward Deployment

This chapter examines some of the elements involved in releasing and deploying code. The chapter begins with an overview of managing configuration files as code. Doing so provides the same benefits as source code management (SCM) in creating a centralized repository that contains the necessary files for a project or service. When considering DevSecOps, managing configuration as code is fundamental to shifting left. Configuration files can be used across environments, from development to production.

The chapter continues with coverage of containerization, specifically Docker. Containerization facilitates a decoupled, microservice architecture, where testing and deployment are inherently reproducible. As with managing configuration as code, containerization makes repeatability quick and easy. The same configuration and container that is deployed in dev can be deployed into test and production. Finally, the chapter briefly describes the blue-green deployment strategy and next steps involved in moving an organization forward in DevSecOps maturity.

Managing Configuration as Code and Software Bill of Materials (SBOM)

Code created by developers as part of a project is managed using an SCM tool like Git. Managing code with an SCM tool enables tracking changes to the code as new features are added and bugs are fixed. At its most basic, code is simply a text file, regardless of the language in which the code is written. Code written in Rust, Perl, Pascal, or any language begins life as a text file.

Just as source code is a text file, so too are the files that configure the behavior of services in a modern infrastructure. For example, the configuration file for a web server such as nginx or Apache is a text file with specific syntax and keywords that determine how the server will behave, the port that it will listen on, the sites available, and other behaviors. Just like source code changes, configuration of services also changes as new features are added and as changes are requested from developers or other similar reasons for a configuration change. Managing configuration files using an SCM has the same benefits as managing source code. Changes can be tracked across time, managed using deployment tools, and rolled back to a known-good version if needed.

Structuring repositories for configuration files varies significantly depending on the operating environment and infrastructure. For example, there may be quality assurance environments that need some of the same configuration file content as the production environment, with the exception of things like credentials for production databases and hostnames, among others.

One method for repository structure involves storing configuration files per environment. This structure can lead to configuration files that unintentionally differ. For example, if a change is necessary within the web server configuration in a testing environment, that change will need to be manually propagated to other environments. If that change is not included, then it might lead to downtime for other environments as the project moves toward production.

A per-application repository structure can be used to alleviate the environmental concerns with per-environment repositories. For example, managing a web server configuration with the top level as *webserver* and using branching and tagging for changes to the file takes advantage of the strength of the SCM plus the simplicity of a single file. The result is that when a new version of the file is needed for a project, that file can be tagged. As the project moves through development to testing to production, that tag can be intentionally used as the configuration. Consider this directory structure:

```
configs/
    webserver/
        common/
        host-specific/
    databaseserver/
        common/
        host-specific/
    firewall/
        common/
        host-specific/
```

An example of a file that would be stored within the *common* web server configuration directory is the *apache2.conf* file found on Debian installations that contains common configuration items and references to other configuration files and directories:

```
Mutex file:${APACHE_LOCK_DIR} default
PidFile ${APACHE_PID_FILE}
Timeout 300
```

```
KeepAlive On
MaxKeepAliveRequests 100
KeepAliveTimeout 5
User ${APACHE_RUN_USER}
Group ${APACHE_RUN_GROUP}
HostnameLookups Off
ErrorLog ${APACHE_LOG_DIR}/error.log
LogLevel warn
IncludeOptional mods-enabled/*.load
IncludeOptional mods-enabled/*.conf
Include ports.conf
<Directory />
    Options FollowSymLinks
    AllowOverride None
    Require all denied
</Directory>
<Directory /usr/share>
    AllowOverride None
    Require all granted
</Directory>
<Directory /var/www/>
    Options Indexes FollowSymLinks
    AllowOverride None
    Require all granted
</Directory>
AccessFileName .htaccess
<FilesMatch "^\.ht">
    Require all denied
</FilesMatch>
LogFormat "%v:%p %h %l %u %t \"%r\" %>s %O \"%{Referer}i\" \"%{User-Agent}i\"" \
    vhost_combined
LogFormat "%h %l %u %t \"%r\" %>s %O \"%{Referer}i\" \"%{User-Agent}i\"" combined
LogFormat "%h %l %u %t \"%r\" %>s %O" common
LogFormat "%{Referer}i -> %U" referer
LogFormat "%{User-agent}i" agent
IncludeOptional conf-enabled/*.conf
IncludeOptional sites-enabled/*.conf
```

The elements found in the *apache2.conf* file can be deployed to any web server being deployed. For example, adding an additional field to the logfile format to capture the IP address from which the request was received is sometimes necessary when using load balancing or cloud providers. In that case, a new `LogFormat` directive would be added and would contain the `%{X-Forwarded-For}i` directive. Also note the use of the `%D` option, which records the time taken to serve the request. This value can be important as you move through deployment to track whether a new change has changed the response time. The directive could be added to the *apache2.conf* file so that the format is available to any virtual host using that same *apache2.conf* file:

```
LogFormat "%h %l %u %t \"%r\" %>s %b \"%{Referer}i\" \"%{User-Agent}i\" %D %v \
    %{X-Forwarded-For}i" xforward
```

However, there may be specific configurations for different servers and microservices within the infrastructure. The configuration files needed for individual sites or types of servers are stored in *host-specific* directories. For example, within the *host-specific* directory, there might be separate directories for the configuration related to the public-facing web server, an authentication web service, and a product web service, with others based on the organization and the web servers being used:

```
host-specific/
    public-web/
    authentication-ws/
    product-ws/
```

A configuration file for a web server from a default Debian install is an example of an application-specific configuration that benefits from the hierarchy:

```
<VirtualHost *:80>
        ServerName www.example.com
        ServerAdmin webmaster@localhost
        DocumentRoot /var/www/html
        ErrorLog ${APACHE_LOG_DIR}/error.log
        CustomLog ${APACHE_LOG_DIR}/access.log combined
</VirtualHost>
```

Within this configuration file, which would be found within the *public-web/* directory, we'll use the ServerName configuration. That option would be different for the authentication web service server found in the *authentication-ws/* directory. The ServerName, DocumentRoot, ErrorLog, and CustomLog directives would change:

```
<VirtualHost *:80>
        ServerName ws-auth.example.com
        ServerAdmin webmaster@localhost
        DocumentRoot /var/www/ws-auth
        ErrorLog ${APACHE_LOG_DIR}/ws-auth-error.log
        CustomLog ${APACHE_LOG_DIR}/ws-auth-access.log combined
</VirtualHost>
```

When placed under SCM, such as Git, any changes to these configuration files would be tracked. This enables rollback and history capabilities. However, the structure shown does not address per-environment differences, such as the differences found between a development environment and its production counterpart.

Details related to testing environments can be handled in two ways, depending on the level and sophistication of automation involved in the process. A manual process involves creating another layer of directories within each of the application-specific directory structure, one for each environment, such as:

```
host-specific/
    public-web/
        dev/
        internal-test/
        integration/
        user-qa/
        production/
    authentication-ws/
        dev/
        internal-test/
        integration/
        user-qa/
        production/
```

As I previously noted, the drawback to the per-environment structure is an increased chance of configuration skew or substantive differences between environment configuration. For example, you may need to add more verbosity to logging in a development environment, or performance tuning options might be enabled in development and test. In this scenario, you'd add a configuration change only to the appropriate nonproduction environment, and it would not be propagated to the configuration files used for other environments. The next project that moves through the pipeline toward production may accidentally include the debugging option, thus causing problems that are unrelated to the project being moved to production. The hope is always to "remember" to remove that extra debugging, but hoping doesn't always work.

Avoiding configuration skew is the goal. Achieving that goal leads toward additional levels of automation and variable-based configuration management. The configuration files are stored in a source code–managed repository, but instead of hardcoding values, any environment-specific information is gathered at time of deployment. Many modern configuration management tools have the necessary capabilities to build dynamic configuration files.

Configuration files are part of a deployment of software, typically in the form of a series of packages that need to be installed together to make an application work. A software bill of materials (SBOM) is used to track dependencies and create a secure software supply chain. An SBOM contains information about each software component, such as the name of the supplier or creator of that software component, the name of the component itself, the version and other identifiers of the software, dependency tracking for this component, and information about the SBOM itself.

An SBOM can be used to verify and validate each piece of a larger application. When a vulnerability is released, it's possible to use the SBOM to verify whether the vulnerable component is used within the application. See "Securing the Software Supply Chain" (*https://oreil.ly/dfiBv*) for more information on SBOM and other practices related to software security.

Using Docker

Docker provides for containerization of applications. Containerization, whether using Docker or another tool, is one of the primary tools that helps organizations move toward automated DevSecOps. Containerizing sometimes requires a paradigm shift away from monolithic, all-in-one applications toward small, purpose-built micro-applications that do one thing and one thing only. While the term "microservices" is popular, the term "micro-application" can be helpful when trying to conceptualize the shift from a larger application to one comprised of smaller applications.

The following sections provide an overview of Docker, including important concepts and some vocabulary. Note that I've written the upcoming material with the assumption that you are familiar with virtualization and some cloud-based concepts. If you are approaching everything fresh, the Docker documentation (*https://docs.docker.com*) and tutorials (*https://www.docker.com/101-tutorial*) are quite good. However, if you are attempting to integrate existing infrastructure and the concepts related to that infrastructure into a containerized world, then this section should be helpful.

Container and Image Concepts

A container is a collection of resources that is used as a computing environment. You might think of a container as a virtual machine insofar as there is abstraction of hardware resources into software. With a container, the compute resources are executed from a file on a filesystem, known as an image. The image contains the operating system and software to be virtualized. Just as virtual machines can be isolated when needed or have access to shared resources, containers can utilize shared disks and other resources on the network.

The paradigm shift toward containerization occurs at a higher level, in how containers are constructed and their intended use. Whereas creating a virtual machine typically involves installing a base operating system from an installer, a container is constructed from an image that already exists. In other words, the typical use case for Docker and other containerization technologies does not include the installation step but rather uses an image of a virtual machine that someone else has installed.

The security-minded and operations-minded may note that using an image of an operating system that someone else has installed is inherently flawed because there is no way of knowing what's on the image or whether the binaries and other files have been modified or tampered with. The counterargument is one of scale and many eyes, meaning that if one of the base container images for Docker was tampered with, the community would be made aware immediately.

From an operational standpoint, the highest performance is obtained when the operating system is installed in a purpose-built manner. The only software on the server is the minimum necessary to accomplish the task of that server. Taking performance a step further, compiling custom binaries of base software like a web server optimizes the system for its purpose. Compiling the kernel itself can also enhance performance.

In an automated, cloud-based world, obtaining this next level of performance is reserved for the highest-need, busiest applications, where microseconds matter. Most business-line, customer-facing applications won't need that type of performance, though, and therefore a shared container image provides performance that's good enough for most needs. The greater performance gains are found through horizontal scaling, strategic regional caching, and data flattening. As performance gains begin to diminish through scaling or other means, an inward focus on core infrastructure can yield additional performance.

Those familiar with virtualization concepts will note that you could use a template or snapshot to mirror the image-to-container experience. In those terms, think of the image being the snapshot. Many virtual machines can be cloned and built from one snapshot in a virtualized infrastructure, and many containers can be built from an image in a containerized infrastructure.

Another concept that differentiates containers from virtual machines is longevity. Virtual machines may be purpose-built but are used in a hosted manner. For example, a virtual machine is built and a version of code is uploaded to that virtual machine and tested there. The virtual machine continues in its current state, awaiting the next version of code to be uploaded and tested.

With a container, the image and software are gathered at runtime, tests are executed, and the container stops. Put another way, the container runs only when there are tasks to execute. It is this concept that can be a stumbling block when learning Docker from a virtualized perspective. Docker makes it easy to download and run an image, but, depending on the image, the container may run and then exit immediately. In a virtual server scenario, the virtual server would continue to run and an administrator would log in to the container to perform configuration and related tasks.

If you need persistence between executions of a container, then you should create a volume. A volume is akin to disk space that is mounted within the container on each execution. Data that changes on the volume is maintained in a frozen state until next use, much like turning a computer off. The data stored on disk is persistent, as is the data stored in a Docker volume.

Obtaining Images

Prior to running a container, you'll need to download an image. In Docker terms, this is known as a "pull." Images can be sourced from a number of locations but most commonly from Docker Hub or from a local registry. This section examines both.

Docker Hub

Docker Hub is an official online registry for images that is integrated with the release of Docker. Docker Hub contains images created by Docker and also the wider community, both vendors and individual contributors alike. Docker Hub is the place to start when learning Docker because you can download a tutorial image and container to begin learning in a hands-on way.

Alpine Linux is a popular variant of Linux used on Docker. Alpine provides a very small installation of Linux and is available on Docker Hub by searching for Alpine. As Figure 5-1 shows, there are numerous Alpine-related images available.

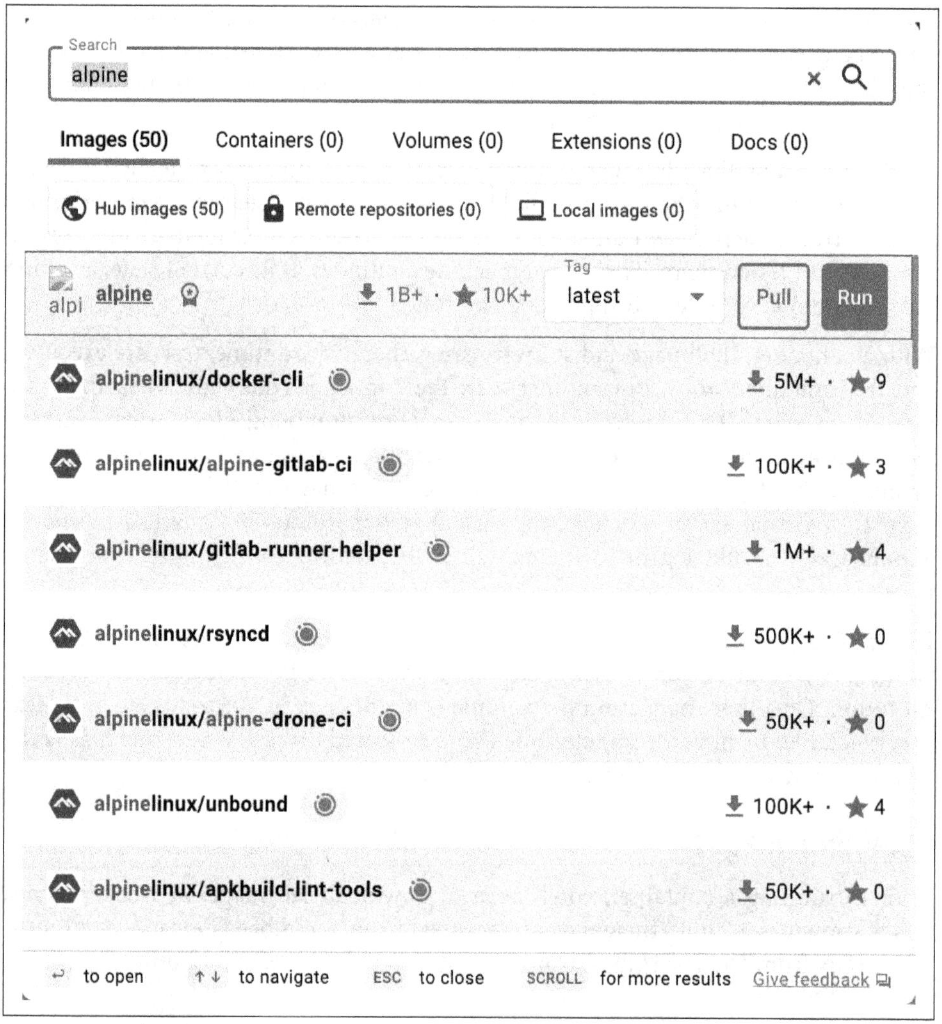

Figure 5-1. The Alpine Linux images available on Docker Hub

The top hit, which has been downloaded over one billion times, has the small ribbon next to it (shown in Figure 5-1 next to the result for "alpine"), indicating that it is a Docker Official Image.

Clicking Pull downloads the image, whereas clicking Run downloads and then executes the image. Running the image reveals the "Run a new container" dialog, shown in Figure 5-2.

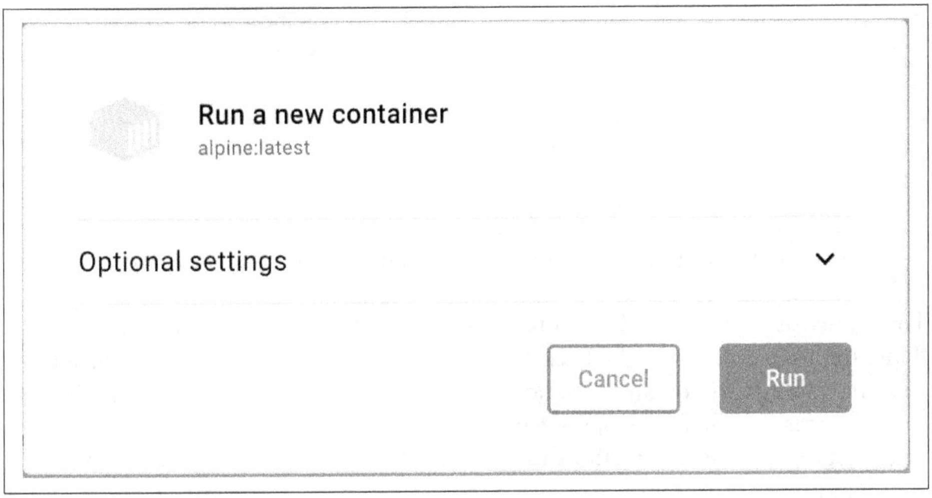

Figure 5-2. Running the container

Clicking Run again executes the image in a new container. Docker will choose a random name for the container. If you'd like to customize the name, click on "Optional settings." For now, I merely clicked Run, which brought up the Containers page, showing the new container (randomly named *blissful_greider*) and showing the status of the container. This is illustrated in Figure 5-3. In addition to the name, whether named manually or randomly, a container identifier (ID) is also produced. This string of characters enables a canonical method for accessing the container.

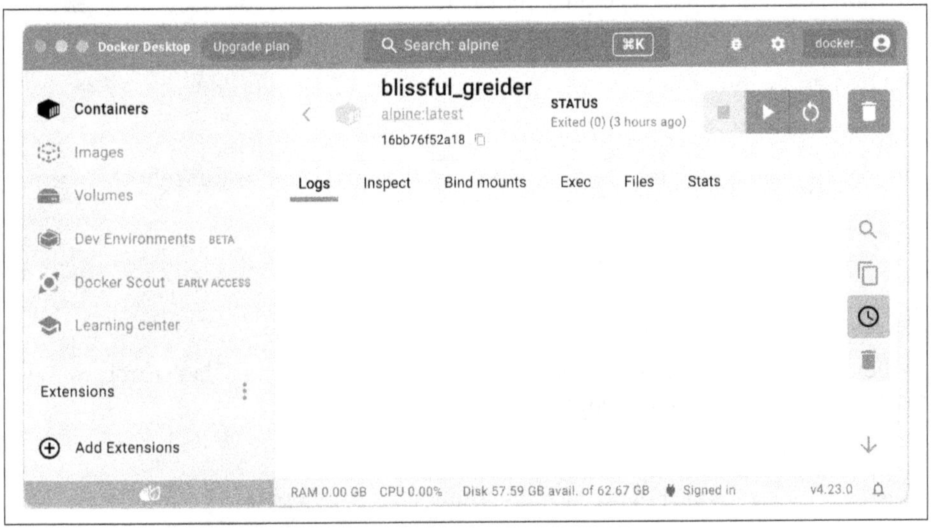

Figure 5-3. Displaying a container and its status in Docker Desktop

As Figure 5-3 shows, the container has exited. The status indication is located in the upper right, and in case it's difficult to read, Figure 5-4 shows that upper-right section zoomed in closer.

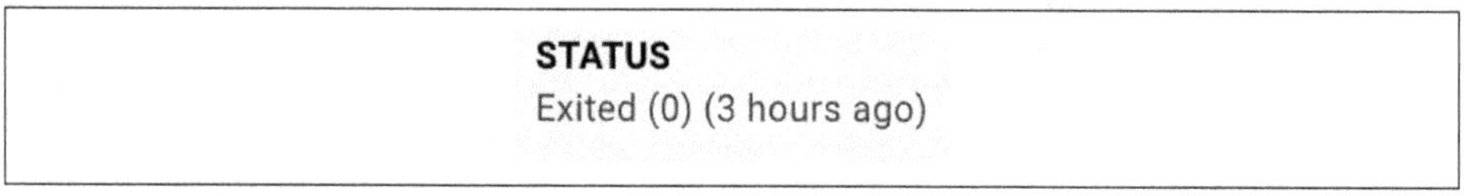

STATUS
Exited (0) (3 hours ago)

Figure 5-4. Zoomed version of the status that is shown for a container in Docker Desktop

The status of a container is a notable difference from a virtual machine. Rather than continuing to run in the background, the container has stopped because there were no more tasks to run. Put another way, a virtual machine would continue to run, whereas a container stops when there are no more processes to run. In the next section, I'll show a method for keeping the container running and allowing command-line or terminal access.

Using the Docker command

While Docker Desktop is an excellent interface for managing images and containers, the cool kids use the command-line interface (CLI) for interacting with Docker. As with just about everything else, the command line makes computer work faster and more efficient. Docker-related commands begin with the docker command, followed by a subcommand and usually some options. Typing docker from the command line (Terminal on macOS/Linux or command prompt on Windows) reveals the various subcommands and options. Typing docker followed by a subcommand will generally display context-sensitive help for that subcommand. Let's take a look at an example.

Run this command:

```
docker search
```

The docker command will then display help that is related to the search subcommand:

```
"docker search" requires exactly 1 argument.
See 'docker search --help'.
Usage:  docker search [OPTIONS] TERM
Search Docker Hub for images
```

Earlier, Figure 5-1 showed the results from a search for alpine. That search can also be performed from the command line with:

```
docker search alpine
```

Doing so displays the list of images containing the word "alpine":

```
NAME            DESCRIPTION       STARS OFFICIAL
alpine          A minimal Docker... 10315 [OK]
alpinelinux/do  Simple and light... 9
alpinelinux/al  Build Alpine Lin... 3
```

```
alpinelinux/gi  Helper image con...   4
alpinelinux/un                        4
```

The results are divided into columns. The first column is the name of the image. The second column contains a description. The third column indicates the number of times that the image has been starred. This is a good indication of the popularity of the image. The fourth column provides an indication of whether the image is an official image, released by Docker. In the listing shown, the first result is the *alpine* image, which has been starred 10,315 times and is flagged as being an official image.

 There is also a fifth column titled AUTOMATED, which is not shown but indicates whether the image can be used as part of an automation workflow.

You can also filter based on whether the official flag is true or false, based on the number of stars that an image has obtained, or based on whether the automated flag is true or false. In the example shown, filtering only for official images looks like this:

```
docker search alpine --filter is-official=true
```

After logging in with the login subcommand, you can download or pull the image:

```
docker pull alpine
```

The image can be executed into a container with:

```
docker run alpine
```

Just as the pull step can be skipped through the Desktop, so too can this step be skipped from the command line. Instead of running docker pull first, you can simply execute docker run and Docker will download the image if needed prior to running it.

Also similar to the behavior of Docker Desktop, when running a container from the command line, Docker will choose a name for the container and will also use default values for other parameters. You can change these parameters through the command line or the Desktop interface. The optional settings available when running a Docker container through Docker Desktop are limited. However, many more options are available through the command line. For example, running a container while manually setting the name while also allocating a terminal, running the container in the background, and allocating a pseudo terminal is accomplished with this command line:

```
docker run --name ch5contain -dit alpine
```

This command uses a friendly name of *ch5contain* rather than the randomly chosen name. The command also uses the -d option to detach from the command line or run in the background. The -i option indicates that standard input (STDIN) should be kept open and interactive. The -t option allocates a pseudo TTY (teletypewriter), which enables command line access within the container itself.

The ps subcommand shows container status:

```
docker ps
```

A list of running containers is returned. In the case of the previous docker run command, the output from docker ps is:

```
CONTAINER ID IMAGE  COMMAND   CREATED   STATUS      PORTS   NAMES
28ae7048c1d3 alpine "/bin/sh" 8 min... Up 8 min...          ch5contain
Assuming that a pseudo TTY has been allocated (using the -dit options shown earlier),
you can connect to a shell prompt within the container using the attach subcommand
followed by the container ID. For example, the container ID
of the container that was just created begins with 28ae7048c1d3. Connecting, or attaching,
to that container is accomplished with the following command:
docker attach 28ae7048c1d3
```

The result is a shell prompt, as the root or superuser, located at the root of the filesystem in Alpine Linux. From there, commands are then within the container, remembering that any changes made within the container filesystem will not persist after the container process stops.

You may also be able to connect with the following command:

```
docker exec -it <container_id> /bin/bash
```

This command will explicitly run a shell within the container.

If you're familiar with working through the command line in Linux, you may be tempted to type "exit" to end your terminal session. However, typing "exit" within the Alpine Linux Docker container that is running a shell will stop the container process. Instead of typing "exit," use the Ctrl-P + Q escape sequence to effectively exit from the terminal without stopping the container process entirely.

The start subcommand is used to restart the container:

```
docker start ch5contain
```

Alternatively, you could also use the container ID:

```
docker start 28ae7048c1d3
```

See the documentation for information related to the Getting Started tutorial (*https://docs.docker.com/get-started*) that is available with Docker Desktop.

Using a local network registry

With the ability to run a container in the background, you can create a local registry, if needed. There are two primary reasons for hosting a local Docker registry. First, an organization can create its own custom containers that are only shared within the organization itself. A second reason to host a local registry is to be able to work semi-offline or in a semi-disconnected state. If the internet connection is down, containers and images can continue to be pulled from the local registry. The focus of this section is creating a locally hosted registry that can be accessed by others within your organization.

The core of a local registry is the aptly titled *registry* image from Docker. You will also need to allow connections to the container, which is accomplished using the -p option at runtime. Depending on the level of security needed, you may also choose to use SSL to encrypt registry-related communication between the local client machine and the local registry server, and you may also choose to add authentication for the registry as well.

The following commands assume that there is a local server that will be used as a central location for Docker images within the organization. The examples use a virtual machine running Debian Linux. Docker was installed on the Debian instance using the instructions in the Docker documentation (*https://docs.docker.com/engine/install/debian*).

While this isn't the place to argue the efficacy of using SSL for communication that occurs over wires within a building, adding the SSL capabilities isn't too cumbersome. The most cumbersome or time-consuming part of adding SSL to the local registry is obtaining an SSL certificate. If the organization does not already have a certificate available, then a self-signed certificate can be generated for use with the local registry.

If you have a valid SSL certificate signed by a recognized certificate authority (CA), then you will not need to run the openssl command shown later. Subsequent examples assume that you have the public and private certificates within a directory structure called *docker/ssl* located within your current directory on the server that will be used as the registry.

If you're using a self-signed certificate, create a directory to hold the certificate and key, and then generate the certificate pair. The newly created certificate and key will be stored in a directory on the host computer called *docker/ssl*. This path is relative to the directory from which you ran the mkdir command. You might consider creating an absolute path on the host computer, such as */etc/ssl/*, for storing the certificate and key.

Note also that the openssl command shown uses a hostname that I created for this example (*dockreg.braingia.org*). Change that hostname and domain for your organization:

```
mkdir -p docker/ssl

openssl req -x509 -nodes -days 365 \
    -subj "/C=US/ST=WI/O=Book/CN=dockreg.braingia.org"
    -addext "subjectAltName=DNS:dockreg.braingia.org" -newkey rsa:4096 -nodes
    -keyout docker/ssl/example.key -out docker/ssl/example.crt
```

You can also add authentication for another layer of security on a local registry. As with adding SSL, authentication is easy to add to the container. On the registry server, generate an *htpasswd* file containing credentials for each user who will access the registry. This is accomplished with the following command. The username will be *reginald*, and the password will be *regpass* in the command. Change according to your needs:

```
mkdir -p docker/auth && cd docker/auth

docker run --rm --entrypoint htpasswd registry:2.7.0 \
    -Bbn reginald regpass >> htpasswd
```

At this point, you've generated a private key and certificate file for SSL and you've created an *htpasswd* file for authentication. These files are located on the server and placed within the *docker/* directory, located within your home directory on that server. Certificate-related files are located in *docker/ssl*, and the authentication-related file is located within *docker/auth*. Docker itself has been installed on the server and is running.

The next step is to make those files available within the container at runtime. The easiest option is a *bind mount*, which is a filesystem that exists on the host machine and gets mounted into the container. With a bind mount, you specify the location of the local file or directory and you also specify the location where that directory will be mounted in the container. For example, if you wanted to make the local *docker/ssl* directory available within the container in a directory called */ssl*, you could do so with this option:

```
-v ./docker/ssl:/ssl
```

It's worth noting that the example shown uses the *./* path to indicate that the path is located in the current directory. You can also use `pwd` (note the run quotes, or backticks) as in:

```
-v `pwd`/docker/ssl:/ssl
```

When the container is running, the contents of the *docker/ssl* directory on the local computer is then available to the container process in a directory called */ssl*.

With the certificate and key created, the next step is to trust them on each of the client computers that will access the registry. The instructions for doing so are specific to the operating system and version of that operating system that you're using. For example, on a Mac you will go to Applications → Utilities → Keychain Access and import an item, selecting the certificate that you created on the registry server. If you executed the `openssl` command, then you'll need to transfer the certificate to each client computer (copy and paste the contents of the *.crt* file, for instance). If importing into a Mac client, be sure to select "Always Trust" to avoid an error regarding an unknown CA. See the Microsoft documentation (*https://learn.microsoft.com/en-*

us/aspnet/core/security/docker-https?view=aspnetcore-8.0) for an overview of working
with Docker and certificates on Microsoft Windows.

 You may see advice or instructions for adding an "insecure registry" option. If you have imported and trusted the certificate, then
you will not need to follow that advice or instruction.

All of that background work leads to finally being able to run the container for the
local server-based registry.

Several environment variables are used to configure the local registry for HTTPS and
authentication. Environment variables are exported using the -e option to the docker
run command. The necessary environment variables for this example are described in
Table 5-1.

Table 5-1. Docker environment variables for HTTPS and authentication

Variable	Description
REGISTRY_AUTH	The type of authentication to be used.
REGISTRY_AUTH_HTPASSWD_REALM	The realm for authentication. This value would typically be displayed in the authentication dialog.
REGISTRY_AUTH_HTPASSWD_PATH	The location of the *htpasswd* file, relative to the container process.
REGISTRY_HTTP_ADDR	Provides the IP address and port on which the registry will be found. Use in combination with the -p option to actually listen on the port as well.
REGISTRY_HTTP_TLS_CERTIFICATE	Path to the public certificate used for SSL communication with the registry. This path is relative to the container itself, not the host computer.
REGISTRY_HTTP_TLS_KEY	Path to the private key used for SSL communication with the registry. This path is relative to the container itself, not the host computer.

The final command uses the -d option, indicating a detached process, and uses the
--restart=always option so that the container runs (or restarts) automatically. The
name of the container is set to *registry*. This is followed by two -v options to create
bind mounts. Each of the environment variables described in Table 5-1 is included.
The container will listen on the default port for HTTPS (TCP port 443). Because of
this, the docker process on the server needs to be executed with sudo or executed as
root:

```
sudo docker run -d --restart=always --name registry \
  -v `pwd`/docker/auth:/auth -v `pwd`/docker/ssl:/ssl \
  -e REGISTRY_AUTH=htpasswd -e REGISTRY_AUTH_HTPASSWD_REALM="Example Registry" \
  -e REGISTRY_AUTH_HTPASSWD_PATH=/auth/htpasswd -e REGISTRY_HTTP_ADDR=0.0.0.0:443 \
  -e REGISTRY_HTTP_TLS_CERTIFICATE=/ssl/example.crt \
  -e REGISTRY_HTTP_TLS_KEY=/ssl/example.key -p 443:443 registry:2.7.0
```

The local server-based registry process should now be running, the certificate should be trusted on client computers that will access it, and at least one user should have credentials to the registry server.

Log in to the newly created registry server with the docker login command, followed by the hostname. For example, if the registry is named *dockreg.braingia.org*, then the command is:

```
docker login dockreg.braingia.org
```

You will be prompted for the username and password. If you used the command shown earlier in this chapter for creating the *htpasswd* file, then the username is *reginald* and the password is *regpass*.

To upload an image to the local registry, you must first download or pull that image to your local computer. For example, to store Alpine Linux on the local registry server instead of needing to retrieve it from Docker Hub every time, you run the following commands. As before, the commands use *dockreg.braingia.org* as the hostname. Change that hostname for your environment:

```
docker pull alpine
docker tag alpine dockreg.braingia.org/alpine
docker push dockreg.braingia.org/alpine
docker rm alpine
docker rm dockreg.braingia.org/alpine
docker pull dockreg.braingia.org/alpine
```

You may note the docker rm commands. The commands remove the locally cached versions; neither command removes the images from the upstream servers.

From this point, the locally hosted registry server will have the *alpine* image. The image can be pulled by others in the organization. At this point, hopefully you have already started managing configuration as code. You could create a directory within your Git repository called *docker*, and within that directory you could store the contents of both the *ssl* and *auth* directories. I also suggest creating a *readme.txt* file or even a Markdown-formatted *readme.md* file to store the commands that you ran in order to get the local registry working.

This section demonstrated pulling from and pushing to a local Docker registry. The local registry contains authentication information, and all data is protected in flight by SSL. More complex scenarios for scaling authentication can be found in the registry documentation (*https://docs.docker.com/registry/#considerations-for-air-gapped-registries*) on the Docker website. It is also relevant that certain container images are marked as nondistributable. Luckily, the most useful container images are not limited in such a way. Regardless, if you need to work around a nondistributable image, you can find instructions for doing so on the Docker website.

Deploying Safely with Blue-Green Deployment

Deploying code to the next environment is the focus of this section. The "next environment" can be anything from basic initial system testing following developer commit/push all the way to and including the production or live environment. As code progresses from developer workstation to production, the potential impact of a problem in the code increases. Therefore, safe deployment is needed. You can use additional tools like Kubernetes to enhance deployments by providing a means to manage containers across providers.

Blue-green deployment is a strategy for moving code through environments in a safe manner by using two sets of infrastructure. The current production environment is noted as the blue environment, while the to-be-production environment is the green environment. Assuming that no problems are identified with the green environment, production traffic can be pointed toward the green environment with the new code. The deployment cycle repeats with the next project coming through the deployment pipeline. Traffic is switched to the new environment after it has been tested.

Obviously, automated testing becomes even more important when moving toward continuous integration/continuous deployment (CI/CD). Tools like Jenkins can help with the CI/CD aspects involved in managing a DevSecOps pipeline. However, even before continuous deployment is integrated, some form of monitoring needs to be in place for the production application.

Monitoring, or being able to verify that requests are being fulfilled successfully and in a timely manner, should be in place even without blue-green deployment. Chapter 6 looks more closely at monitoring.

Summary

This chapter provided an overview of best practices around configuration file management using an SCM tool like Git. The chapter also promoted the use of containerization techniques for facilitating a DevSecOps CI/CD deployment pipeline. Included in that section was coverage of Docker, although other containerization software and tools can also be used. Finally, I provided a brief overview of blue-green deployment, noting the importance of automated testing and monitoring while progressing on a DevSecOps path.

The ideas behind configuration as code have been around for decades but more formally expressed as such relatively recently. I distinctly remember managing DNS zones with CVS before Git was created. The move toward containerization started quite some time ago as well. Migrating entire applications to containers can take time and courage because of inherent danger when decoupling monolithic applications. Technical debt that has been incurred over the years while maintaining that monolithic app gets repaid in a hurry, all while hoping that some behind-the-scenes cyclical activity that runs only once every four years wasn't hidden away in that application. No amount of DevSecOps will help for that case.

The focus of the next chapter is deployment and monitoring. The chapter uses Jenkins as a base for demonstrating the concepts surrounding deployment. Some might argue that Jenkins is not modern enough for new DevSecOps organizations. However, Jenkins conveys the concepts of deployment in a consistent way that is stable, reproducible, and accessible for readers. In addition, Jenkins has the advantage of being mature and able to integrate with legacy technologies that frequently are the most urgent platforms in need of migration to DevSecOps.

## CHAPTER 6

Deploy, Operate, and Monitor

By the time an application reaches the production environment, the code behind that application should have been reviewed and tested multiple times and in multiple ways. The deployment of the code, whether in a container, in the cloud, or a combination of legacy, cloud, and container, should have been done multiple times, leaving little room for surprises when the code was promoted to the production environment. This shifting left of work is a central theme of DevOps and DevSecOps. Deploying, operating, and monitoring in a repeatable manner very early in the software development lifecycle (SDLC) helps DevSecOps practitioners to discover problems earlier rather than later, when the problems are less impactful to timelines and end users.

This chapter looks at CI/CD with the idea that automated CI/CD is a goal that is first achieved on the left side of the SDLC before moving into quality assurance and production environments. The chapter also highlights monitoring as a contributing factor in the success of DevSecOps.

Continuous Integration and Continuous Deployment

The level of complexity needed for deployment of a modern application has increased significantly over the past two decades. In many organizations, no downtime can be incurred as a result of needing to deploy an application to the production environment. Where a deployment might have occurred in the wee hours of the morning, causing backend applications like the database servers to go down while the schema was changed, now feature flags and blue-green deployment are normal.

This section starts with building and maintaining environments with Ansible and then demonstrates the use of Jenkins for deployment. We'll use Jenkins to build a simple but extendable code delivery pipeline. Some organizations will have matured into multicontainer environments. Those organizations may outgrow the deployment model and software demonstrated in this chapter. For instance, organizations using Kubernetes may utilize something like Argo CD or another deployment tool. In addition, organizations using multiple cloud providers may use cloud native tools or an integration of multiple tools as part of their DevSecOps processes. Both the number of software tools and the number of potential combinations of software tools needed makes it impossible to cover in a single book, much less a single chapter. Therefore, my goal is to demonstrate the process through a real-world example that is extendable to other tools as DevSecOps matures within an organization.

Building and Maintaining Environments with Ansible

Ansible is one of a handful of technologies that helps with automation of complex infrastructures, including bare metal deployment of an entire application stack. Ansible differs in that it is lightweight, can operate in an agentless manner, and uses plain-text configuration file formats such as YAML and INI. Ansible uses SSH and Python. That makes one less attack vector, agent software, in favor of standardized software such as SSH that's installed or available on modern operating systems.

Ansible operates around the concept of inventories and playbooks, where an inventory defines the devices being managed by Ansible and the playbook defines the desired state of the device. For example, a group of servers that need to have DNS-related configurations applied to them might be grouped as such:

```
[dns_servers]
dns1.example.com
dns2.example.com
dns3.example.com
```

You could then install DNS-related software and customized configuration using Ansible. For example, a list of tasks could be created for these hosts:

```
---
- name: ensure installed- bind9
  apt: name=bind9 state=present
- name: sync named.conf
  copy: src={{ config_dir }}/dns/named.conf
       dest=/etc/bind/named.conf group=bind backup=yes
  notify:
    - restart named
  tags:
    - bindconfigs
```

I've shown two configuration options within this example, ensuring that the BIND DNS server is installed and then synchronizing the configuration file by copying it over to the device under management. The `apt` command will be used for the installation, and Ansible enables a `state` to be set for the package. In the example shown, the value for `state` is `present`, meaning that Ansible will install the software if it's not there already. But this `state` attribute also effectively means that if you wanted to ensure that certain software was uninstalled or not present, a simple change to the value of `state` will ensure that the software is not present.

The other configuration option shown in the example takes a local file (*named.conf*), found in the directory defined as *{{ config_dir }}* (a local variable that you can create), and copies the file to a destination within */etc/bind* on the remote device. Group ownership is set for the file, and a backup copy of the file is made on the remote device, just in case changes have been made to that file on the remote device. Numerous other options, such as setting the permissions and user ownership, among other things, can be done with the `copy` module as well.

Using Ansible, you can create a desired state for environments in a DevSecOps infrastructure and then deploy to those environments with a single command, `ansible-playbook`. From a security perspective, Ansible and other automation tools facilitate a known-state. The same configurations can be used to verify that the server is using a known-good set of configurations for its services.

Ansible provides the underlying, repeatable infrastructure support that DevSecOps teams need. Other software can be used for specialized line-of-business application deployment beyond the service configurations that Ansible provides. Jenkins and similar software are used for deployment of line-of-business application code, and conveniently enough, the next section covers Jenkins.

Using Jenkins for Deployment

Jenkins is an automation service written in Java that can connect many disparate parts of a modern application into a single coherent deployment. Jenkins is both powerful and extensive in its ability, and entire careers can be made out of simply training others on Jenkins. Therefore, this section will be limited solely to the creation of a pipeline for deployment of an application. The deployment can be built out further and extended into a more complex architecture.

Overall, the architecture includes a Debian server running Docker. This server is responsible for the local registry built in Chapter 5. That Docker server will orchestrate builds with Jenkins by also running a Jenkins container. The server does not need to run Debian, but I recommend creating a server that will be responsible for DevSecOps tools. This may turn out to be more than one server, depending on your needs. However, rather than trying to configure Jenkins on a local computer and then migrating to a server, it will be easiest and fastest to simply install a server, whether virtual or real, that will run container processes.

Jenkins can be installed as a Docker container. When doing so, you will need to include persistent storage so that the Jenkins configuration details remain available even if the container process ends. Using the *dockreg* server we built in Chapter 5, you can install Jenkins using this command:

```
mkdir jenkins_home
docker run -v ./jenkins_home:/var/jenkins_home -p 8080:8080 -p 50000:50000 \
    --restart=on-failure --name=jenkins jenkins/jenkins:lts-jdk17
```

This will download and run a container for Jenkins, listening on port 8080. The directory *jenkins_home* will be made available as */var/jenkins_home* within the container. When the image is downloaded and the container begins to run, a password will be displayed to the console/terminal window:

```
*************************************************************
*************************************************************
*************************************************************
Jenkins initial setup is required. An admin user has been created
and a password generated.
Please use the following password to proceed to installation:

8629142b85534c39924a45150eaa7fe5
This may also be found at: /var/jenkins_home/secrets/initialAdminPassword
*************************************************************
*************************************************************
*************************************************************
```

That password is used for the administrator account, called admin, and you'll need to remember it until you can change it. The path to the password is also included, just in case you forget it. The path shown is relative to the container.

With the container installed, the next step is to connect to Jenkins using a web browser. Point the browser toward the IP or hostname of the server where the container is running, on port 8080. For example, I have installed the Jenkins container on the Debian server that I used in Chapter 5, called *dockreg.braingia.org*. Therefore, the URL to which I point the browser is:

```
https://dockreg.braingia.org:8080/
```

Figure 6-1 shows the initial screen, prompting for the password for the admin account.

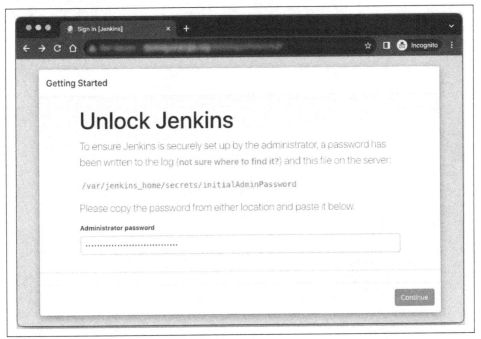

Figure 6-1. Logging into Jenkins for the first time

On first run, Jenkins will prompt whether to install common plug-ins or whether to customize the list of plug-ins that will be installed; see Figure 6-2.

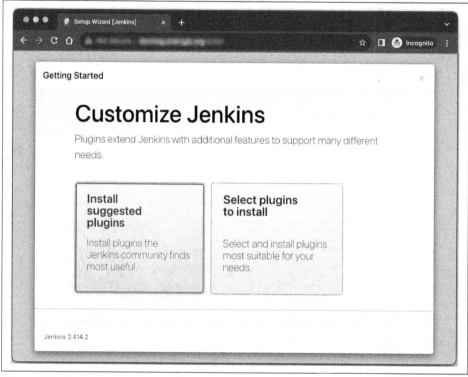

Figure 6-2. Choosing the suggested plug-ins as a starting point for Jenkins

The suggested plug-ins are a good starting point until you've had a chance to determine which plug-ins are needed in your infrastructure. Figure 6-3 shows the plug-ins being installed on the Jenkins container deployed as part of this chapter.

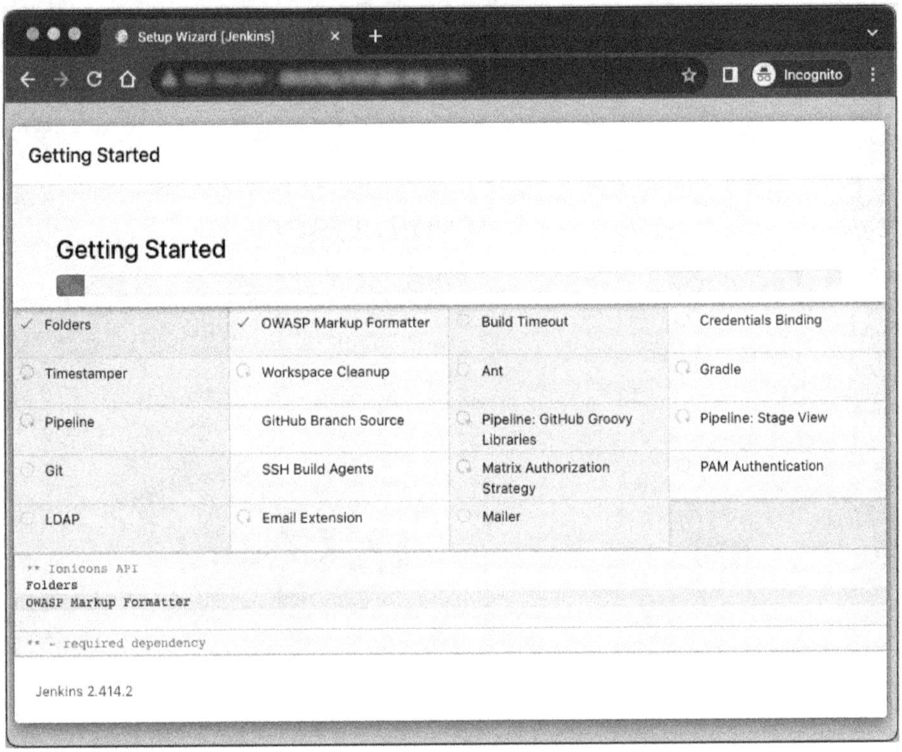

Figure 6-3. On first run, Jenkins can install some common plug-ins

Next, the Setup Wizard for Jenkins prompts you to create a new user rather than using the admin account. Figure 6-4 shows this screen. You can also choose to skip the creation of an admin user and just continue as the normal admin account.

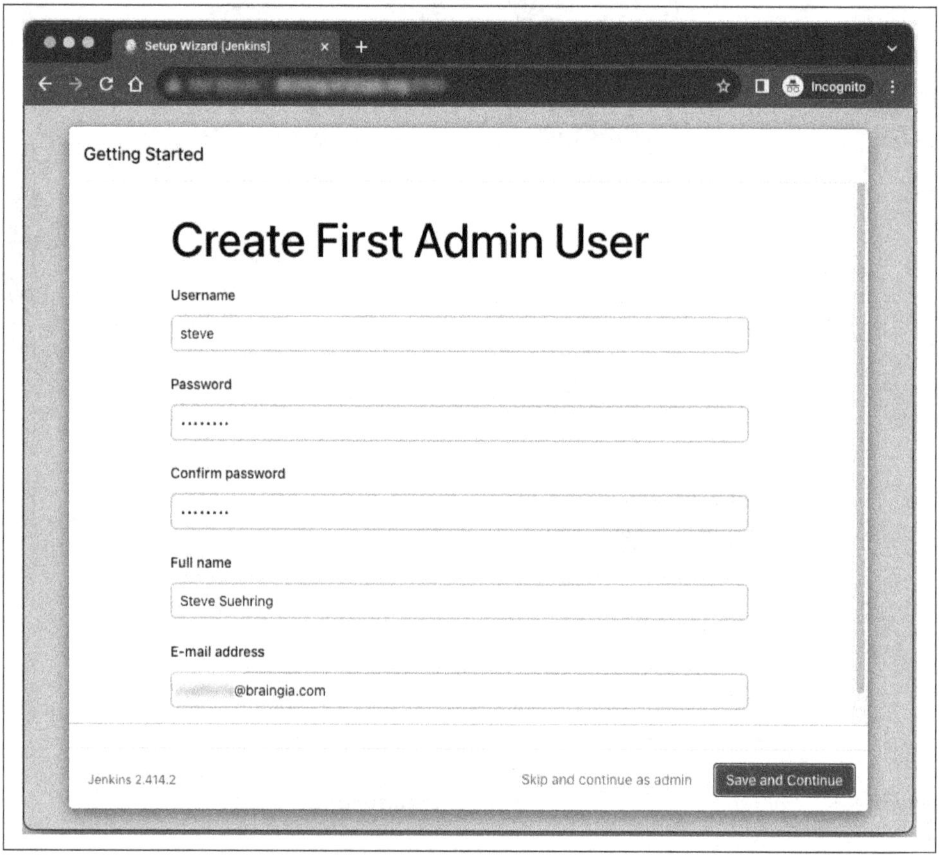

Figure 6-4. Creating an admin user within Jenkins

You'll see the Instance Configuration screen next, which is shown in Figure 6-5. In this case, the default value was fine. However, if you did not have a DNS name or needed to change the port due to being behind a proxy or load balancer, this would be the location to make that change.

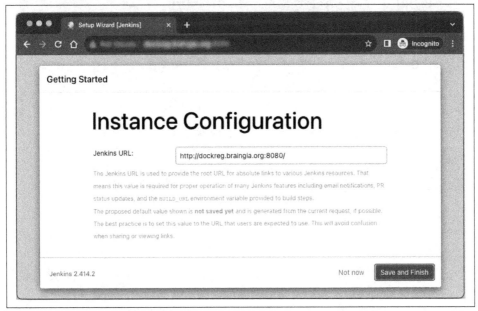

Figure 6-5. Configure the URL for Jenkins within the Instance Configuration screen

Clicking Save and Finish reveals the success screen, shown in Figure 6-6. Click "Start using Jenkins" to proceed to the Jenkins dashboard.

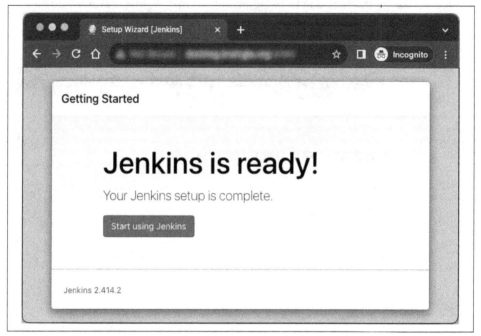

Figure 6-6. This screen is shown when the Setup Wizard is complete

Figure 6-7 shows the Welcome to Jenkins page. After you've created a job or started to work with Jenkins, this dashboard will display the status of those jobs along with other relevant information. The next section includes details on creating a job.

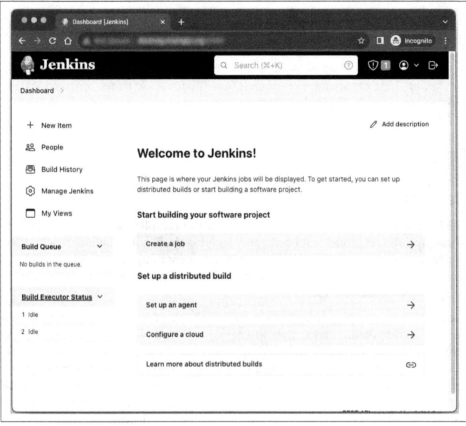

Figure 6-7. The Jenkins dashboard is used to find out current job status and administer the Jenkins server

On future executions of Jenkins through Docker, you may find it beneficial to start in detached mode. To do so, you'll first need to stop the Jenkins container and then remove it. From another terminal window, stop the container with the following command:

```
docker stop jenkins
```

Note that this assumes you've used the --name option and that the name of the container is *jenkins*. If you didn't use the --name option or if the container is called something different, then you'll need to adjust the command accordingly. You can always use the canonical container ID, which can be found with the docker ps command.

With the container stopped, you can remove the container with this command:

```
docker rm jenkins
```

Next, running in detached mode adds the -d option, and the entire command becomes:

```
docker run -d -v ./jenkins_home:/var/jenkins_home -p 8080:8080 -p 50000:50000 \
    --restart=on-failure --name=jenkins jenkins/jenkins:lts-jdk17
```

If you're running in detached mode and need to view the logs or console output, use the docker logs command. For example, assuming the container is named *jenkins*, this command would display logs from that container:

```
docker logs jenkins
```

As a reminder, you can see the names of the running containers with the docker ps command.

Creating a Pipeline

The internet tubes are overflowing with examples of complex pipelines using Jenkins. These pipelines pull code, build code, and deploy code. But the complex pipelines are also quite specialized. Rather than adding unnecessary complexity, this section shows how to create a simple pipeline with Jenkins. The example can be extended to add the complexity necessary for your infrastructure.

Even with the goal of creating a simple example, there are a few initial tasks that need to be completed. This example will deploy a file to a web server. While that may sound trivial, the foundation of many deployments is moving files between servers securely. If the source file was located on a different server or hosted through Git, then we'd need to add a step to first retrieve the file. If the source code needed to be built, then we'd add a step to build. Transferring the files to the destination is nearly always needed, though, and thus represents a logical place to begin.

The transfer will use the could use the rsync command as well, especially in cases where there are multiple files. The scp command relies on underlying SSH infrastructure such as host key exchange and authentication. In an automated deployment scenario, key-based authentication is used to move files because doing so does not require manual intervention.

By default, the "home" directory of Jenkins is */var/jenkins_home*. This filesystem is hosted on the local server and then exported or mounted to the container. Therefore, you can interact with and make changes to files even if the container is not running. One such change is to create a .ssh directory—note the dot preceding the name—within the *jenkins_home* directory. If you've been following earlier examples, there will be a directory called *jenkins_home* within your current directory, likely within your own home directory.

SSH, and by extension `scp`, attempts to verify the host key of the server to which you are connecting. A file called *known_hosts* is then used to store the host keys of servers to which you've connected and accepted the host key. When copying files between servers in an automated manner, a person is not present to type "yes" or "no" to indicate whether to accept or reject the host key.

Failure to account for the host key verification step will result in an error indicating that the host key verification failed, shown in Figure 6-8 from Jenkins.

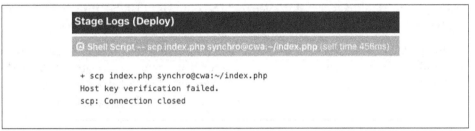

Figure 6-8. Host key verification failed because the SSH host key was not known to the Jenkins user

While there are numerous methods for working around host key verification and also for transferring the host key, I've found that copying the key is frequently the lesser of two evils. That method is not without its drawbacks. First, manually accepting the key once does not scale well for anything above maybe three servers, although you may have a higher tolerance for the mundane. More importantly, in an automated DevSecOps world, you may not know the host key until deployment time.

When deploying a new server as part of a release, the deployment tooling can obtain a copy of the host key. This key can be placed into the *known_hosts* file, simply as another step in the deployment process. Therefore, in the interests of moving forward with a simple example, I will describe how to manually copy the key, knowing that these steps can be automated later.

From the host server running the Jenkins container, make an SSH connection to the destination server. For example, I would like to deploy the website to a server named *cwa*, but I need to obtain the key for that server. Therefore:

```
ssh cwa
The authenticity of host 'cwa (192.168.1.4)' can't be established.
ED25519 key fingerprint is SHA256:4sYWNFdOU812rc/vh5150yQbfWE+Y6/1C/0ANuBs0Nik.
This key is not known by any other names.
Are you sure you want to continue connecting (yes/no/[fingerprint])? yes
Warning: Permanently added 'cwa' (ED25519) to the list of known hosts.
```

That key will be added to the *known_hosts* file within my own *.ssh* directory. But I need to place the contents of that key into the *known_hosts* file in the *jenkins_home/.ssh* directory. The first step is to create the *.ssh* directory in *jenkins_home*:

```
mkdir jenkins_home/.ssh
```

Next, open *~/.ssh/known_hosts* with a text editor or simply the `cat` command and copy the key into a new *known_hosts* file. The file will be located in *jenkins_home/.ssh/*. As an alternative, you could also brute-force all of the *known_hosts* from your home directory into the version found in the *jenkins_home/.ssh* directory. I don't generally recommend that, because doing so will overwrite the *known_hosts* file for Jenkins, which could have unintended side effects.

At this point, you should have a *jenkins_home* directory that contains many other files and directories, including a new directory that you just created called *.ssh*. Within the *jenkins_home/.ssh/* directory should be a file called *known_hosts*. The contents of the *known_hosts* file should be the host key of the server to which you'll connect.

Next, there needs to be a method for authentication as it relates to the `scp` command. This involves ensuring that the Jenkins user has a valid SSH key and that the key exists in the *authorized_keys* file for the user on the server to which files will be copied. In the example we're building for this chapter, there is a user called *synchro* that is located on the *cwa* server.

We need to generate a key pair for the Jenkins user and place the public key within the *authorized_keys* file on *cwa* for the *synchro* user. The following command generates the key (this command is executed on the server running Jenkins, *dockreg.braingia.org* in this example):

```
ssh-keygen
```

Assuming the default values are accepted, the `ssh-keygen` command will generate two files, *id_rsa* and *id_rsa.pub*. You should place both of these files within *jenkins_home/.ssh/*, and both should have limited permissions:

```
cp ~/.ssh/id_rsa* jenkins_home/.ssh/
chmod 600 jenkins_home/.ssh/id_rsa*
```

 If you're unfamiliar with key-based SSH authentication or how to create a key, see "How to Use ssh-keygen to Generate a New SSH Key?" (*https://www.ssh.com/academy/ssh/keygen*).

Pipeline creation begins by giving the pipeline a name and choosing the type (Pipeline) from the Jenkins New Item screen. This is shown in Figure 6-9.

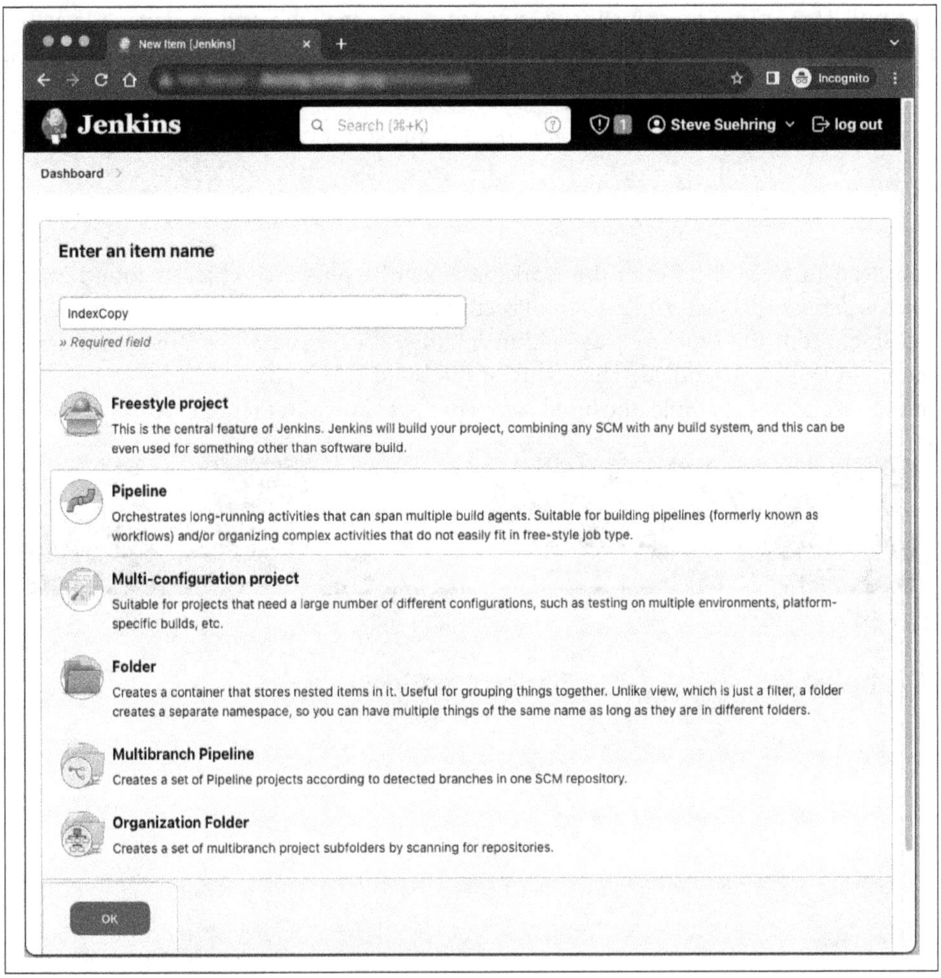

Figure 6-9. Creating a pipeline in Jenkins

Within Figure 6-9, I have used the name *IndexCopy* and selected Pipeline. I will then click OK. The General configuration page for the pipeline will be displayed. Scroll to the bottom of the page to reveal the Pipeline section. Within the Pipeline section, place the following:

```
pipeline {
    agent any
    stages {
        stage('Deploy') {
            steps {
                sh "scp index.php synchro@cwa:~/web/index.php"
            }
        }
    }
}
```

The only step within this pipeline is to execute the `scp` command to copy a file called *index.php* to a server named *cwa* as the username *synchro*. The file will be placed in a directory called *web* located within the home directory for the *synchro* user.

The last step is to create the *index.php* file. The file should contain:

```php
<?php
print "Index Page";
?>
```

You need to place the file in the workspace for the pipeline, which is found in the *jenkins_home/workspace/IndexCopy* directory. With that done, you can execute the pipeline. From the Pipeline page within Jenkins, click Build Now. When you do so, the build will be scheduled. The status of the build will be displayed on completion. In the case of this example, the build succeeded, as shown in Figure 6-10.

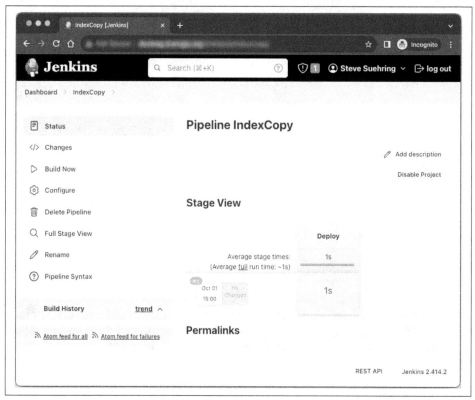

Figure 6-10. A successful build within Jenkins

When working with Git, there is an option found within the Manage Jenkins → Security page that configures how to handle keys. This is shown in Figure 6-11. However, for other use cases and tools, we need another method for handling host keys.

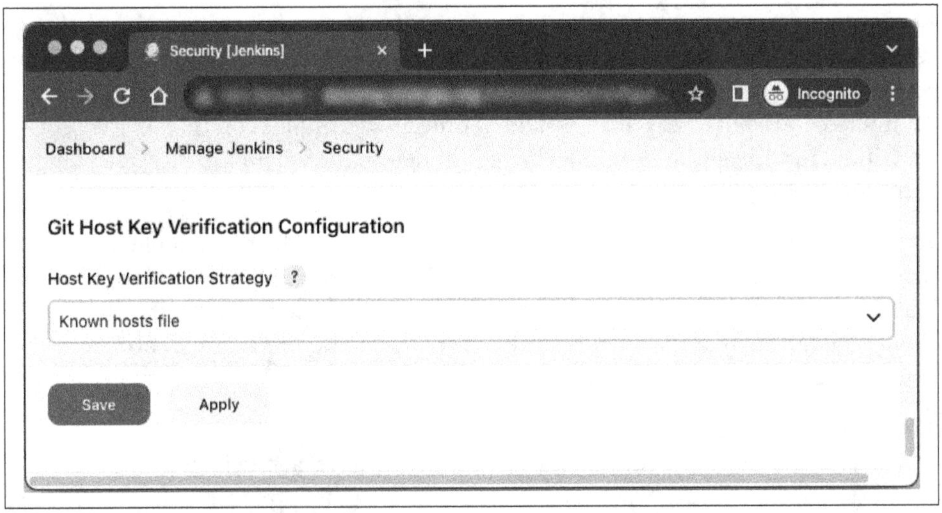

Figure 6-11. Configuring the host key management strategy for Git within Jenkins

If your build did not succeed, you can view the logs by hovering over the red- or green-shaded box on the Pipeline page and selecting Logs. Figure 6-8 from earlier in this chapter is a log view created when I had placed the *known_hosts* file in the wrong location due to an errant mistyped path.

With a single deployment complete, you can now extend into multiple steps to build an entire orchestrated end-to-end deployment from environment to environment. When backing up the configuration related to Jenkins, the Jenkins job information is found in the *jenkins_home/jobs/ hierarchy*.

Jenkins has plug-ins for popular cloud providers like AWS, Azure, Google Cloud Platform, and others. You can add pipeline tasks to deploy to EC2 instances on AWS, for example. As currently configured, the pipeline needs to be started manually. This is a step but not the final answer for CI/CD in DevSecOps. Instead, the pipeline should be kicked off automatically, triggered by a code commit or other milestone that then not only builds the infrastructure but also deploys the code itself. The final stage is automated switching of the production workloads toward the newly deployed code. To achieve that goal, you'll need to make sure monitoring is in place.

Monitoring

The level of complexity needed for deployment of a modern application has increased significantly over the past two decades. In many organizations, no downtime can be incurred as a result of needing to deploy an application to the production environment. If that sounds familiar, then you obviously read the introduction to the previous section.

Keeping complexity under control is a constant challenge. Meeting the challenge requires visibility throughout the deployment and operational cycle of an application. For example, knowing that last week the average response time for a request was 41 milliseconds but today that response time is 484 milliseconds, the DevSecOps practitioner can begin to examine changes to determine where the increased latency is coming from.

Among the tools available for monitoring are everything from a simple `ping` command to complex cloud-based monitoring suites. Whereas Docker, Kubernetes, and Jenkins have mindshare, if not market share, in their respective areas, there is no one single monitoring tool that stands above all. With that in mind, this section examines some best practices for monitoring:

Visibility generally means fixability

If you can see an issue occurring, then you have a much greater chance of addressing the issue when compared with a random report that an end user called in to the help desk. Having worked in the industry from Level 1 tech support through technical architecture, I'm convinced that many technical problems could be fixed if the correct person examined the problem. Too often, the answer is "Turn it off and then back on again" when that "solution" should rarely be needed.

At the DevSecOps level, knowing that there is a problem before the tech support call center starts lighting up can shorten the time for a fix to be implemented. For example, seeing an entire regional data center suddenly go offline enables traffic and workloads to be shifted quickly while the cause of the outage is investigated.

Triage is important

Using the data center suddenly disappearing from the internet as an example, it may not be you or anyone on your team who will ultimately reconnect the fiber that was cut and caused the data center to go offline, but it can be you who shifts that traffic and works around the problem. Likewise, if there is a spike in calls about slowness of application response time, knowing that the shifting of traffic could cause a slowdown for others will help to identify the issue as related but unimportant.

It's a triage mentality that can be helpful when outages happen. The help desk ticket about uploading a photo that affects one user is less important and should receive less attention than the backhoe cutting through the fiber-optic communication cable and the resulting need to reroute traffic. Finding the root cause of an outage may take time. If workarounds are available, you should consider those with the goal of reducing impact on end users and meeting service-level agreements.

Shift downtime left with instrumentation enabled

As alluded to in the introduction to this chapter, shifting left is a core DevOps and DevSecOps philosophy. Problems that might have only occurred when the project was deployed to production can occur earlier in the SDLC, in earlier non-production environments. If problems arise in a nonproduction environment, those problems will necessarily be less impactful than if they occurred later in the lifecycle of the code.

Further, you can enable instrumentation in the form of additional debugging and logging in the nonproduction environment. Not only can the additional visibility help solve problems, but it can also help spot issues that may otherwise have been hidden. Take care not to leave additional logging enabled in the production environment. Aside from potentially leading to poor performance, there could be regulatory impacts if things like personal or credit card information are captured in a production environment.

Focus on important metrics

Not every metric is equal. Knowing the disk input/output (I/O) latency for a database server is an important metric related to its performance. The disk I/O for a firewall should be less important than the network interface throughput, though. That doesn't mean disk I/O should not be recorded for the firewall but that focusing on disk I/O for the firewall may lead the team on the wrong troubleshooting path.

With that in mind, focusing on the overall goal and how the individual metrics contribute to that goal is the important element of monitoring key metrics. The number of requests that can be serviced per second and the time taken to service a request are two metrics for a web server. Knowing that there are numerous contributing factors such as disk I/O, compute, memory, and network latency can help direct any efforts toward correcting problems.

Don't forget dependencies

Network latency is a good example of an area where a false alert can occur. If the web server was responding to a ping in 38 milliseconds and is suddenly now responding in 2,842 milliseconds, any number of issues could be the root cause. If there are two routers and a wide area network (WAN) link between the monitoring computer and the web server, then knowing that a router is causing the issue would be important. Therefore, using related metrics where possible can help pinpoint whether there is an issue worth investigating or whether the upstream provider has an issue.

Alerts need to be actionable

One of the worst experiences of my career occurred at an employer where part of the job was being after-hours/late-night on call. The employer had a scheduled job that ran overnight on one of the legacy systems, and every night after 11 p.m.

that system would send out a message indicating that the job completed. Not that the job completed abnormally, just that the job completed. There was no task that needed to happen as a result of that alert.

I spoke with my manager regarding the nightly alert, and they indicated that the alert was sent by design so that we would know that the job completed. If the job didn't complete or encountered an error, then I would need to alert someone else so they could stop other jobs from running. What happened next was like the scene from the movie *Spinal Tap* where Nigel explains that his amp goes to volume "11" and Marty asks why they couldn't just make volume "10" be that much louder. You can see the wheels turning for Nigel, but ultimately he points out that this amp goes to 11. In much the same way, I pointed out that we should just alert if the job doesn't complete correctly and then only alert the person that needed to fix the issue. After briefly contemplating that vexatious thought, my manager assured me that the alert was needed and was working as designed.

Alerts need to be actionable. If an alert is not actionable, then just record it in a logfile or somewhere else that makes sense for your infrastructure. In this context, actionable means that as a result of receiving the alert, I need to do work, usually on a computer, to correct the cause of the issue. If the alert comes through and I don't need to do anything, then the alert should've been muted until I sought it out or until it became actionable.

Locating the difference between actionable and nonactionable can take time, and I usually err on the side of getting a nonactionable alert until I figure out where that threshold is located. As time goes by, the action-to-noise ratio needs to lean heavily toward actionable. Every alert that comes through means something is actually wrong and I'm the right person to fix it.

This section covered some of the elements involved in monitoring within DevSecOps. Adding visibility through logging and instrumentation is one of the more helpful additions in a DevSecOps organization. Monitoring key performance metrics including their dependencies facilitates the left-shift needed to move toward DevSecOps capabilities. Alerting only on actionable issues enables everyone to focus on core issues and improve the overall deliverability of an application.

Summary

This chapter focused on operating and monitoring, including deployment of an application. The chapter began with detailed coverage of Jenkins for creating a reproducible CI/CD strategy. Jenkins was deployed as a Docker container with persistent storage. The basic ideas behind DevSecOps monitoring wrapped up the chapter. These include enabling as much logging and instrumentation as possible, as early as possible, to promote visible infrastructure. Visibility enables problems to be found earlier in the application development lifecycle. All the while, keep in mind that adding logging and instrumentation can sometimes have performance implications. The trick is to find the right balance between logging and using all of the disk space in the world. There reaches a point where being able to trace backward through a user interaction is not realistic or helpful because the user has since rebooted or done something else to fix or at least temporarily fix whatever issue was being encountered. Monitoring key performance indicators in aggregate form can be helpful, though. Knowing that response times have suddenly doubled would be something worth noting, and then having logging automatically enable itself after that threshold so that a human can look at the issue later would also be nice!

Looking ahead, Chapter 7 shows a means for expanding the efforts around containerization with a demonstration of Kubernetes. While there are countless Kubernetes demonstrations, many of those tutorials and demonstrations assume that you have a lot of background in Kubernetes already. The aim with Chapter 7 is to show a simple implementation such that you might build on it as you learn more about Kubernetes and where it fits within the DevSecOps journey.

Plan and Expand

The previous chapter introduced and reinforced concepts around configuration management, deployment, and monitoring. The focus of this chapter is on expanding beyond development-related processes and into scaled-up deployments. The speed with which DevSecOps deployment-related technology is moving makes it difficult to justify printing instructions for its use. Therefore, my primary goal for this chapter is to demonstrate the current state of one of the more mature products, Kubernetes. Reaching that goal means creating a Kubernetes installation, which is where the chapter begins.

Scaling Up with Kubernetes

Docker helps to move application development from a virtual server or cloud-based server infrastructure toward a service-based, process-level paradigm where individualized microcomponents and microservices make up a larger application. Kubernetes takes this shift even further by providing scalable container management. Kubernetes helps with application-level scaling, container orchestration, and ultimately microservice architectures at scale.

Coming from a physical server or virtual server to Kubernetes may appear as overkill at first, when some of the same solutions can be found with Docker Compose. However, Kubernetes provides a level of abstraction that would be cumbersome with Docker Compose when deploying thousands or tens of thousands of servers. By the end of the section, you will have a running Kubernetes cluster with two worker nodes.

Understanding Basic Kubernetes Terms

The architecture of Kubernetes is divided into a control plane and worker nodes. The control plane contains several services such as a key/value store, an application programming interface (API), a scheduler, and a controller manager. The controller manager is responsible for node and job management, among other duties. On the nodes, an agent called a kubelet ensures that containers are running, while a proxy called kube-proxy is responsible for network communication. The container runtime also runs on a node. Together, a collection of containers is known as a "pod" in Kubernetes, and the term "cluster" is used to describe the collection of services that constitutes an entire Kubernetes installation.

Kubernetes also defines Services (note the uppercase "S") in a special way. A Service in Kubernetes can be thought of as a network-based listening service, like a web server.

Installing Kubernetes

Creating a working Kubernetes can be challenging at first. I recommend using a virtual server template or base installation of a Linux distribution that you can revert back to and start over without needing to install the operating system again. This section uses Debian 12 as its base operating system. The goal is to create an expandable cluster manager along with two nodes. The primary controller will have a hostname of *k8s*. The first worker node will be named *k8s-node1* and the second named *k8s-node2*. Either add those hosts to your local DNS server or add them to the */etc/hosts* file on each of the machines involved. Those names are used as part of the configuration process and within Kubernetes. Therefore, a prerequisite step before continuing is to set up the hostnames.

Kubernetes requires several operating system–level changes, including disabling swap and the usage of overlay networking. Assuming you've installed Debian, the following two commands (executed as root) will turn off swap and permanently disable it on restart:

```
swapoff -a
sed -i '/ swap / s/^\(.*\)$/#\1/g' /etc/fstab
```

Create a modules load file for containerd with the following two commands:

```
echo overlay >> /etc/modules-load.d/containerd.conf
echo br_netfilter >> /etc/modules-load.d/containerd.conf
```

Next, load the modules immediately:

```
modprobe overlay
modprobe br_netfilter
```

Kernel options need to be added through `sysctl`. Create a file called *99-k8s.conf* within the */etc/sysctl.d* directory. The file should have the following contents:

```
net.bridge.bridge-nf-call-iptables = 1
net.ipv4.ip_forward = 1
net.bridge.bridge-nf-call-ip6tables = 1
```

Run the `sysctl` command as follows to effect the changes just made to the file:

```
sysctl --system
```

Next, begin installing software. There will be two rounds of software installation:

```
apt update && apt -y install containerd curl \
    gnupg gnupg2 software-properties-common
```

You'll need to make a configuration change manually to the containerd configuration file. But first, you'll create the configuration file with this command:

```
containerd config default > /etc/containerd/config.toml
```

Edit the configuration file */etc/containerd/config.toml*. Within the file, locate the following line:

```
SystemdCgroup = false
```

Change the value to `true`. When complete, the line should look like this:

```
SystemdCgroup = true
```

Save the file and restart and enable containerd:

```
systemctl restart containerd
systemctl enable containerd
```

Next, obtain the key so that you can install the software using the Debian `apt` command. Note that you may need to change the version from v1.28 to the latest version (or whatever version you're trying to install):

```
curl -fsSL https://pkgs.k8s.io/core:/stable:/v1.28/deb/Release.key | \
    gpg --dearmor -o /etc/apt/keyrings/kubernetes-apt-keyring.gpg
```

Add the repository with the following command, changing the v1.28 version if needed to match the previous command:

```
echo 'deb [signed-by=/etc/apt/keyrings/kubernetes-apt-keyring.gpg] \
    https://pkgs.k8s.io/core:/stable:/v1.28/deb/ /' | \
    tee /etc/apt/sources.list.d/kubernetes.list
```

Update the list of packages and install Kubernetes, marking those packages as "held":

```
apt update
apt -y install kubelet kubeadm kubectl
apt-mark hold kubelet kubeadm kubectl
```

Finally, I recommend rebooting to ensure the changes have taken effect. The previous sentence is something that I never thought I would write in regard to a Linux system. Then `systemd` happened. Rebooting should not be necessary but unfortunately sometimes is necessary when `systemd` is involved. Therefore, reboot. While the system is rebooting, recall fondly the days when Linux servers never needed rebooting and logfiles were plain text and stored in one location. You might also try the command systemctl daemon-reexec instead of rebooting, but I had mixed success with this method, and it really shouldn't be needed but for the inherently flawed architectural decisions that work against the Unix way for no substantive benefit for a server use case.

From this point forward, you will use a normal, nonprivileged user account but will invoke sudo, thus running some commands as a privileged user. If you do not have sudo installed, you can do so with this command:

```
apt install -y sudo
```

See the documentation for *sudoers* for information on how to add your user account to the *sudoers* configuration file.

> The documentation for *sudoers* and many other Linux commands is found using the manual pages, accessed through the man command, as in:
>
> ```
> man sudoers
> ```

With the prerequisite work done and software installed, it's time to initialize the Kubernetes cluster:

```
sudo kubeadm init --control-plane-endpoint=k8s --upload-certs
```

The init subcommand of kubeadm will perform several tasks related to creating the cluster. If this step fails, a possible reason is that the DNS or */etc/hosts* file was not updated to add an address for the host named *k8s*. When complete, you will see output similar to the following:

```
Your Kubernetes control-plane has initialized successfully!

To start using your cluster, you need to run the following as a regular user:

  mkdir -p $HOME/.kube
  sudo cp -i /etc/kubernetes/admin.conf $HOME/.kube/config
  sudo chown $(id -u):$(id -g) $HOME/.kube/config

Alternatively, if you are the root user, you can run:

  export KUBECONFIG=/etc/kubernetes/admin.conf

You should now deploy a pod network to the cluster.
Run "kubectl apply -f [podnetwork].yaml" with one of the options listed at:
  https://kubernetes.io/docs/concepts/cluster-administration/addons/

You can now join any number of the control-plane node running the
following command on each as root:

  kubeadm join k8s:6443 --token n8hb0z.6zzh095e175kskc8 \
    --discovery-token-ca-cert-hash sha256:8a9b[...]c714 \
    --control-plane --certificate-key 0fe7[...]1a19
```

```
Please note that the certificate-key gives access to cluster
sensitive data, keep it secret!
As a safeguard, uploaded-certs will be deleted in two hours;
If necessary, you can use
"kubeadm init phase upload-certs --upload-certs"
to reload certs afterward.

Then you can join any number of worker nodes by running
the following on each as root:
kubeadm join k8s:6443 --token n8hb0z.ezzh095e175kskc8 \
    --discovery-token-ca-cert-hash sha256:8a9b[...]c714
```

Note that the cryptographic elements such as tokens and cert hashes will be different in your output. See "Re-creating the join command" on page 143 if you forget the token or other cryptographic elements. The output is informative of what you need to do next, specifically:

```
mkdir -p $HOME/.kube
sudo cp -i /etc/kubernetes/admin.conf $HOME/.kube/config
sudo chown $(id -u):$(id -g) $HOME/.kube/config
```

Adding networking

You'll need to add a virtual network layer to the Kubernetes cluster. There are several methods for accomplishing this task. This chapter uses Project Calico (*https:// github.com/projectcalico*).

Apply the network layer with the following command:

```
kubectl apply \
    -f https://raw.githubusercontent.com/projectcalico/calico/master/manifests/calico.yaml
```

Alternately, if you experience problems with the previous command, you can download the *calico.yaml* file and apply it locally instead:

```
wget https://raw.githubusercontent.com/projectcalico/calico/master/manifests/calico.yaml
kubectl apply -f calico.yaml
```

The final step is to join other Kubernetes computers to the cluster. You can add those computers as control-plane nodes, thereby creating a full-blown clustered and redundant control plane, or you can add the computers as worker nodes. In either case, the command will be kubeadm join along with several options (shown in the output of the init command executed earlier). To create a control-plane node, add the --control-plane option. The goal of this section is to add two worker nodes, which means that we will not be using the --control-plane option.

Prior to executing the kubeadm join command, each node requires the prerequisite steps shown earlier in this section. I have distilled those commands here with a reminder that two manual steps are required. First, create a file called */etc/sysctl.d/ 99-k8s.conf* containing the configuration shown, and second, edit the containerd configuration file to change the Cgroup to `true`. Both steps are noted with a # comment in the listing:

```
swapoff -a
sed -i '/ swap / s/^\(.*\)$/#\1/g' /etc/fstab
echo overlay >> /etc/modules-load.d/containerd.conf
echo br_netfilter >> /etc/modules-load.d/containerd.conf
modprobe overlay
modprobe br_netfilter
# Create /etc/sysctl.d/99-k8s.conf with the following:
    net.bridge.bridge-nf-call-iptables = 1
    net.ipv4.ip_forward = 1
    net.bridge.bridge-nf-call-ip6tables = 1

sysctl --system
apt update && apt -y install containerd curl gnupg \
    gnupg2 software-properties-common
containerd config default > /etc/containerd/config.toml

#Edit the configuration file /etc/containerd/config.toml:
#    SystemdCgroup = true
systemctl restart containerd
systemctl enable containerd
curl -fsSL https://pkgs.k8s.io/core:/stable:/v1.28/deb/Release.key | \
    gpg --dearmor -o /etc/apt/keyrings/kubernetes-apt-keyring.gpg

echo 'deb [signed-by=/etc/apt/keyrings/kubernetes-apt-keyring.gpg]
        https://pkgs.k8s.io/core:/stable:/v1.28/deb/ /' | \
        tee /etc/apt/sources.list.d/kubernetes.list

apt update && apt -y install kubelet kubeadm kubectl && \
    apt-mark hold kubelet kubeadm kubectl
```

 Note that the `echo` command had to be broken onto multiple lines in the previous code listing. Include everything within the single quotes as one line when entering this command.

With the prerequisites complete, join a worker node with the following command (change the `--token` value and the `--ca-cert-hash` value to match the values shown for your installation):

```
kubeadm join k8s:6443 --token u1ewom.iqk6hefg99y0ivu7 \
    --discovery-token-ca-cert-hash sha256:cc03[...]c714
```

At this point, the node will attempt to contact the cluster control plane. If something goes wrong at this stage, the problem is often hostname related. Attempting to ping the control-plane node from the worker node is a primary (and easy) troubleshooting step. If the control-plane node, which is called *k8s* in the examples here, does not respond, then that is the first issue to correct. If the control-plane node responds to ping on its IP but not by the name *k8s*, then the issue is hostname related.

If successful, you'll see the following output:

```
[preflight] Running pre-flight checks
[preflight] Reading configuration from the cluster...
[preflight] FYI: You can look at this config file with
'kubectl -n kube-system get cm kubeadm-config -o yaml'
[kubelet-start] Writing kubelet configuration to file
"/var/lib/kubelet/config.yaml"
[kubelet-start] Writing kubelet environment file with flags
to file "/var/lib/kubelet/kubeadm-flags.env"
[kubelet-start] Starting the kubelet
[kubelet-start] Waiting for the kubelet to perform the TLS Bootstrap...

This node has joined the cluster:
* Certificate signing request was sent to apiserver and a response was received.
* The Kubelet was informed of the new secure connection details.

Run 'kubectl get nodes' on the control-plane to see this node join the cluster.
```

The next task is to execute the same join command on *k8s-node2*. When complete, you will be able to run kubectl get nodes on the control-plane node and see both of the worker nodes joined to the cluster. As shown in the following output, the status of all three hosts is Ready. The host *k8s* has the control-plane role, while the other two nodes currently have no roles:

```
NAME         STATUS   ROLES           AGE    VERSION
k8s          Ready    control-plane   15h    v1.28.2
k8s-node1    Ready    <none>          74m    v1.28.2
k8s-node2    Ready    <none>          89s    v1.28.2
```

Re-creating the join command

When a Kubernetes cluster is initialized, some important pieces of information are shown, such as the token to join the cluster. If you forget the token or the cryptographic pieces that are shown in the success message, you can re-create those or view them later.

On the cluster controller, run the following command to re-create the join command in its entirety:

```
kubeadm token create --print-join-command
```

You can also obtain individual elements. For example, run the following command to view the token:

```
kubeadm token list
```

Combine the output of the token and the CA certificate hash to create the join command.

Run this command to view the hash:

```
openssl x509 -pubkey -in /etc/kubernetes/pki/ca.crt | \
openssl rsa -pubin -outform der 2>/dev/null | \
openssl dgst -sha256 -hex | sed 's/^.* //'
```

There are quite a few special characters in that command. Take care if you're typing it manually, and also take care if copying and pasting it because sometimes copy and paste will try to be super helpful and change characters on your behalf.

In this section, you installed Kubernetes on Debian, including a control-plane node and two worker nodes. The cluster is managed on the host *k8s*. The cluster is configured in such a way that multiple nodes can take on a control-plane role, thus enabling some redundancy for the cluster and avoiding a single point of failure in the control plane. If you'd like to change a role from worker to control plane, first remove the node from the cluster with the `kubectl drain` command and then reset the node and join the node with the `--control-plane` option added to the `kubectl join` command along with the certificate. The following commands, executed from the control-plane node, are helpful:

```
kubectl drain <node>
```

Alternately, a more thorough and graceful approach adds the following options:

```
kubectl drain <node> --ignore-daemonsets --delete-local-data
```

Delete the node with the command:

```
kubectl delete node <node>
```

On the node itself, run the `reset` command:

```
kubeadm reset
```

When complete, run the `kubeadm join` command again with the `--control-plane` option added.

Deploying with Kubernetes

Containers are deployed as pods within Kubernetes, but the value of Kubernetes comes in its ability to manage deployments or applications as a single unit with redundancy built in. Where you can use Docker Compose to deploy applications as a single unit, Kubernetes adds redundancy in the form of replicas. This section examines Kubernetes deployment of a simple load-balanced application. As with other examples in the book, the goal is to demonstrate an implementation with only a few moving parts, which can then be expanded and customized as needed for your environment.

As with Docker, configuration for Kubernetes is stored in one or more configuration files. Storing configuration as files brings with it the advantages of Configuration as Code found in DevSecOps. Kubernetes configuration files are YAML-formatted.

Defining a Deployment

Consider an application that consists of a web frontend along with web services that then call to data stores. Testing the application involves spinning up web servers and database servers or at least mocked-up versions of those data stores containing test data. When running, the application should always have at least five frontend servers ready to serve client requests, and other microservices ready to service calls to the data stores.

A Kubernetes Deployment (uppercase "D") enables you to define that end state of the application, with as many frontend servers and whatever other components are needed to deploy the application. Kubernetes will ensure that the pods are running and bring in other resources as specified in the configuration file or files.

Using a ConfigMap

Among the many options available with Kubernetes is a ConfigMap. A ConfigMap is a configuration file used to store pod-specific configuration, making that configuration information available within the pod itself. For this simple example, a Config-Map with an HTML page is as follows:

```
apiVersion: v1
kind: ConfigMap
metadata:
  name: configmap-chapter7-1
data:
  index.html: |
    <!doctype html>
    <html>
      <head>
        <title>Deployment 1</title>
      </head>
      <body>
        <h1>Served from Deployment 1</h1>
      </body>
    </html>
```

Within the ConfigMap file, which I will save as *configmap1.yaml*, the kind and data fields are of immediate interest. The kind field indicates that this is a ConfigMap. As you'll see later, other kinds of files exist too. The data field contains an *index.html* file with the contents of a simple HTML web page as plain text. It's also worth noting that the metadata field and associated elements within the metadata field will change in other files but are important to the inner workings of deployments.

Save the file as *configmap1.yaml*. If you haven't worked with YAML before, pay particular attention to tab/whitespace characters. Indenting is everything with YAML.

Creating the Deployment file

The Deployment file is also YAML-formatted. For this example, the Deployment file is as follows:

```
apiVersion: apps/v1
kind: Deployment
metadata:
  name: deployment-chapter7-1
spec:
  replicas: 2
  selector:
    matchLabels:
      app: nginx
  template:
    metadata:
      labels:
        app: nginx
    spec:
      containers:
      - name: nginx
        image: nginx
        ports:
        - containerPort: 80
        volumeMounts:
        - name: config-chapter7-1
          mountPath: /usr/share/nginx/html
      volumes:
      - name: config-chapter7-1
        configMap:
          name: configmap-chapter7-1
```

You'll notice the `kind` field is set to Deployment and the `metadata` field also contains a `name` key, set to `deployment-chapter7-1` in this file. The `spec` field, an abbreviation of the word "specification," is the main part of the deployment configuration. The `replicas` key defines the number of replicas that Kubernetes will attempt to execute at all times. The `selector` key connects elements of a deployment. Kubernetes uses this selector, when present, to marshal various parts of a deployment into a coherent whole.

Within the `template` specification, note the use of `volumeMounts` and `volumes`. These sections connect the deployment to the ConfigMap created earlier in this chapter. Thus, the `name` field `configmap-chapter7-1` needs to match the metadata name found in the *configmap1.yaml* file created earlier.

Save the file as *deploy1.yaml*. The end result of this file along with the *configmap1.yaml* file creates an nginx deployment serving the contents of the HTML that was included in the ConfigMap file.

Running the Deployment

At this point, you can load the ConfigMap and Deployment with the following commands:

```
kubectl apply -f configmap1.yaml
kubectl apply -f deploy1.yaml
```

If everything goes according to plan, you will receive the following output:

```
configmap/configmap-chapter7-1 created
deployment.apps/deployment-chapter7-1 created
```

If you receive errors, there's a good chance that something is wrong in the YAML. Check indenting. When in doubt, retype manually.

Verifying the Deployment

The following commands can be helpful to gain visibility into the current status of a deployment.

View the current status of a deployment:

```
kubectl get deployments
```

View the current status of pods:

```
kubectl get pods
```

View additional information about pods:

```
kubectl get pods -o wide
```

View detailed information about a pod:

```
kubectl describe pod <podname-id>
```

View current status of ConfigMaps:

```
kubectl get configmaps
```

View detailed information about a ConfigMap:

```
kubectl describe configmap <configmap>
```

View all deployments:

```
kubectl get deployments -A
```

Defining a Service

Up until this point, the deployment has not been made available to the outside world or anything beyond localhost. A Kubernetes Service is required for that purpose. Like other parts of the deployment, a Service is defined by a configuration file:

```
apiVersion: v1
kind: Service
metadata:
  name: service-chapter7
spec:
  selector:
    app: nginx
  type: NodePort
```

```
ports:
- name: http
  port: 80
  targetPort: 80
  nodePort: 30515
externalIPs:
- 192.168.1.158
```

As before, note the kind key has changed, this time to Service. Note also the selector field, which matches that from the *deploy1.yaml* file. Finally, note the use of the externalIPs key. In the example, that is set to a specific IP address of the Kubernetes controller. The IP that you set here will almost certainly be different. In some cases, you won't need to define the externalIP, and in other cases that externalIP will be auto-assigned because of the type of service being used.

Save the file as *service.yaml* and apply the file with the command:

```
kubectl apply -f service.yaml
```

At this point, you should be able to go to another computer on the network and reach the deployment through the "external" IP that was defined within the external IPs configuration field. For example, the external IP configured in the example is 192.168.1.158. I have another computer on the same 192.168.1. network. From that other machine, I ran the following command:

```
curl http://192.168.1.158
```

The result was:

```
<!doctype html>
<html>
  <head>
    <title>Deployment 1</title>
  </head>
  <body>
    <h1>Served from Deployment 1</h1>
  </body>
</html>
```

A few things can go wrong that would prevent the curl command from returning the output shown. Troubleshooting begins with the ping command. Rather than attempting an HTTP request, simply pinging the IP address can reveal that basic connectivity is not available. Without being able to ping the IP, HTTP will almost certainly not work (the following note explains why "almost certainly" exists in the sentence).

 The phrase "almost certainly" in relation to the ping command not working is there because the protocol underlying ping, ICMP, may be blocked but TCP connections for serving web pages may be allowed. Therefore, you can sometimes retrieve web pages from an IP address but not be able to ping that IP.

Connectivity may not be available because the pod isn't running or because the network layer is not running. See "Adding networking" on page 141. Finally, the problem could be as simple as having the wrong IP address. The 192.168.1.158 address is a valid private IP address and happens to be how my test network is configured. If your network uses different IP addresses, then the curl command will need to be adjusted accordingly.

Moving Toward Microservices

We've now deployed a web server to serve a static web page. If that seems anticlimactic, it probably is. The year 1996 called and wants its thunder back. In seriousness, we've deployed processes on top of virtual computing that serve web pages and manage themselves. That's at least 2010s magic.

Expanding the problem is one of my three superpowers. Therefore, another Deployment and another ConfigMap will prove out some of the strengths of Kubernetes. This section assumes that you have *deploy1.yaml*, *configmap1.yaml*, and *service.yaml* running correctly.

Create a file called *deploy2.yaml* with the following contents:

```
apiVersion: apps/v1
kind: Deployment
metadata:
  name: deployment-chapter7-2
spec:
  replicas: 5
  selector:
    matchLabels:
      app: nginx
  template:
    metadata:
      labels:
        app: nginx
    spec:
      containers:
      - name: nginx
        image: nginx
        ports:
        - containerPort: 80
        volumeMounts:
        - name: config-chapter7-2
          mountPath: /usr/share/nginx/html
      volumes:
      - name: config-chapter7-2
        configMap:
          name: configmap-chapter7-2
```

Create a file called *configmap2.yaml* with the following contents:

```
apiVersion: v1
kind: ConfigMap
metadata:
  name: configmap-chapter7-2
```

```
data:
  index.html: |
    <!doctype html>
    <html>
      <head>
        <title>Deployment 2</title>
      </head>
      <body>
        <h1>Served from Deployment 2</h1>
      </body>
    </html>
```

Apply both:

```
kubectl apply -f configmap2.yaml
kubectl apply -f deploy2.yaml
```

The *configmap2.yaml* file is referenced within *deploy2.yaml*. Notice that the `<title>` and `<h1>` contents are different in *configmap2.yaml* when compared with *configmap1.yaml*. Notice also that there are 5 replicas configured within *deploy2.yaml*. This effectively means that 2.5 times as many "Deployment 2" pages should be served, although that's not strictly guaranteed.

View the external IP again and reload to see both "pages" being loaded. You'll know that you're receiving the page from this new deployment when you see the `<title>` and `<h1>` contents change:

```
<!doctype html>
<html>
  <head>
    <title>Deployment 2</title>
  </head>
  <body>
    <h1>Served from Deployment 2</h1>
  </body>
</html>
```

You can also execute `kubectl get pods` to see the current state:

```
NAME                                    READY   STATUS  RESTARTS  AGE
deployment-chapter7-1-765bff56bf-gcd4f  1/1     Running    0      31s
deployment-chapter7-1-765bff56bf-v5hxr  1/1     Running    0      31s
deployment-chapter7-2-86cb66499d-bklfx  1/1     Running    0      21s
deployment-chapter7-2-86cb66499d-hcglb  1/1     Running    0      21s
deployment-chapter7-2-86cb66499d-kk4p5  1/1     Running    0      21s
deployment-chapter7-2-86cb66499d-m5qf9  1/1     Running    0      21s
deployment-chapter7-2-86cb66499d-nhvl4  1/1     Running    0      21s
```

If something goes wrong at this level, a typographical error could be to blame. Begin troubleshooting by ensuring that the earlier examples were running. If those examples were not running, then adding more complexity will not usually fix the problem.

Connecting the Resources

You can keep Deployment files and associated ConfigMap, Service, and other related files separate, as in the examples in this chapter. You may also join those files into a single file. You can use and manage other parts like namespaces in the single file or multifile format. An informal and unscientific survey of organization patterns reveals equal numbers of single-file and multifile management.

If you choose to use a single file to manage all elements of a deployment, the different parts of the YAML file need to be separated with three dashes. The final single-file example that includes all resources from this chapter is included here. If you use this single file, be sure to change the value found within `externalIPs` at the end of the file:

```
apiVersion: v1
kind: ConfigMap
metadata:
  name: configmap-chapter7-1
data:
  index.html: |
    <!doctype html>
    <html>
      <head>
        <title>Deployment 1</title>
      </head>
      <body>
        <h1>Served from Deployment 1</h1>
      </body>
    </html>
---
apiVersion: v1
kind: ConfigMap
metadata:
  name: configmap-chapter7-2
data:
  index.html: |
    <!doctype html>
    <html>
      <head>
        <title>Deployment 2</title>
      </head>
      <body>
        <h1>Served from Deployment 2</h1>
      </body>
    </html>
---
apiVersion: apps/v1
kind: Deployment
metadata:
  name: deployment-chapter7-1
spec:
  replicas: 2
  selector:
    matchLabels:
      app: nginx
  template:
```

```yaml
      metadata:
        labels:
          app: nginx
      spec:
        containers:
        - name: nginx
          image: nginx
          ports:
          - containerPort: 80
          volumeMounts:
          - name: config-chapter7-1
            mountPath: /usr/share/nginx/html
        volumes:
        - name: config-chapter7-1
          configMap:
            name: configmap-chapter7-1
---
apiVersion: apps/v1
kind: Deployment
metadata:
  name: deployment-chapter7-2
spec:
  replicas: 5
  selector:
    matchLabels:
      app: nginx
  template:
    metadata:
      labels:
        app: nginx
    spec:
      containers:
      - name: nginx
        image: nginx
        ports:
        - containerPort: 80
        volumeMounts:
        - name: config-chapter7-2
          mountPath: /usr/share/nginx/html
      volumes:
      - name: config-chapter7-2
        configMap:
          name: configmap-chapter7-2
---
apiVersion: v1
kind: Service
metadata:
  name: service-chapter7
spec:
  selector:
    app: nginx
  type: NodePort
  ports:
  - name: http
    port: 80
    targetPort: 80
    nodePort: 30515
  externalIPs:
  - 192.168.1.158
```

If you choose to utilize multiple files for a deployment rather than the single file shown here, I recommend choosing a naming standard for the metadata and the files themselves. It's debatable how to structure or format that convention, whether prefixing with the kind or type of resource or prefixing with the application name so that all resources are grouped together in a listing.

Integrating Helm

In the bad old days when we had to walk uphill both ways to school in the snow, adding software involved downloading a tar archive, typically gzipped. That file would be decompressed and unarchived, and the dance of `./configure && make && make install` followed. If anything went wrong, then removing the *config.cache* file and possibly running `make clean` was next.

Today, the industry uses package managers to install software and dependencies. Everything from *apt*/*dpkg* on Debian and derivatives to Homebrew on a Mac or even entire container images on Docker are managed as packages. So, too, are packages available with Kubernetes through Helm (*https://helm.sh*). Even more meta than package management is that you can use a package manager to install Helm, itself a package manager. The installation process (*https://helm.sh/docs/intro/install*) is covered on the Helm site and can be accomplished across various operating systems.

Helm collects the configuration files and directories into something called a chart. Charts describe the desired state of an application, including all of the prerequisites needed to run it. Charts contain a mix of YAML-formatted files, JSON-formatted files, and optional text files, among others. For example, the typical layout for a chart is described in Table 7-1.

Table 7-1. A typical chart layout for Helm

File/Directory	Description
Chart.yaml	Basic information about the chart itself, YAML-formatted
charts/	A directory that contains dependencies of this chart
crds/	A directory containing custom resource definitions
LICENSE	Optional text file containing license terms
templates/	A directory containing template files that work in conjunction with the *values.yaml*/*values.schema.json* files to generate Kubernetes files
README.md	An optional text file with helpful information about this chart
values.yaml	A YAML-formatted file containing defaults for this chart
values.schema.json	An optional JSON-formatted file that contains structure-related information for the *values.yaml* file

The *Chart.yaml* file itself contains several required fields. These fields are described in the Charts documentation (*https://helm.sh/docs/topics/charts*) on the Helm website.

Helm charts are found in repositories. There is a default repository called the Artifact Hub that gets installed with the Helm package, and new repositories can be added if necessary. Searching the default Artifact Hub repository is accomplished with this command:

```
helm search hub
```

For example, to search for a MariaDB chart, the command is:

```
helm search hub mariadb
```

As of this writing, 52 charts are returned with that search. A current challenge with the interface and structure is that it's difficult to determine which, if any, of the returned charts are official releases or from known/trusted authors. The Artifact Hub (*https://artifacthub.io*) interface on the web helps with this problem. When searching, you can sort by "Stars," which may provide an indication of popularity.

When installed, a chart becomes a release in Helm terms. An installation of a chart that becomes a release can be repeated multiple times. This is a differentiation between Helm and a more common package manager experience. For example, when MariaDB is installed on a computer running Debian, the software is installed just that one time. However, with Helm, a chart can be installed multiple times, thereby creating multiple releases.

Helm can be helpful in facilitating use of Kubernetes and as a kick start to some of the more advanced configurations and software available through Kubernetes as an organization shifts processes to the left.

Summary

This chapter has only scratched the surface of Kubernetes and what it can do for DevSecOps. Cloud integration, backend integration, and dynamic content are three areas to study as you expand use of Kubernetes. Google Cloud is a natural fit for Kubernetes, but AWS and Azure, along with other cloud providers, all play nice with Kubernetes and integrate with hybrid cloud configurations.

The focus of this chapter was expanding DevSecOps by employing Kubernetes. Kubernetes manages significant portions of operational deployment and abstracts several application layers at the same time. Learning to deploy with and troubleshoot Kubernetes will help to shift left processes related to managing service discovery and deployment. The natural progression of DevSecOps within an organization does not end with Kubernetes, but Kubernetes plays a central role in containerized microservice architectures.

Thus far, the book has combined theory and practice, both foundational and current material. The last few chapters emphasized hands-on experience deploying some of the popular tech frequently involved in DevSecOps organizations. The next chapter shifts back toward theory, summarizing many of the paradigm shifts that occur with DevSecOps.

## CHAPTER 8

Beyond DevSecOps

Determining the contents for a book on DevSecOps is more about determining what *not* to put in a book about DevSecOps. The primary problem is the term "DevSecOps" itself. It means different things to different people depending not only on context but also on experience and organizational need. The technology has not matured to the point where a true recipe for success is available. There are patterns to follow and pieces of tech to use—which I'll describe here—but the exact details of what to type and where to type it are impossible to prescribe. Importantly, DevSecOps is not an end goal but rather an iterative improvement process that evolves as new technologies become available that can make software delivery faster and more reliable.

DevSecOps Patterns

This section includes several patterns of success followed by organizations, whether on the path toward DevSecOps or using a mature DevSecOps SDLC:

- Shifting left toward CI/CD
- Multicloud deployments for redundancy
- Less emphasis on post-deployment security; security is shifted left and automatic
- Linux, specifically command-line-based not GUI, but the rest of the stack interchangeable
- Less emphasis on troubleshooting and optimizing in favor of refactor and redeploy

Let's start by discussing shifting left toward CI/CD.

Shifting Left and Adding CI/CD

Continuous integration/continuous deployment (CI/CD) is really the ultimate goal of DevSecOps. A developer should be able to write code and have that code pass through several gates toward the production environment. Getting to true CI/CD requires significant customization of the pipeline.

Software like Argo CD (*https://argoproj.github.io/cd*) is designed with DevSecOps in mind. Argo CD has graphical components to help with visibility but also a modern backend that takes advantage of the tools covered in previous chapters, such as Kubernetes and Helm, among others. You can leverage Argo CD either as is or as a source of information on how to get to a more modern pipeline.

Multicloud Integration

Containerization is the current state of the art in DevSecOps, as of this writing. The three main cloud providers, AWS, Google Cloud, and Azure, all provide containerization that integrates well with Kubernetes, noting that Google Cloud has a natural affinity to Kubernetes due to its history. Running containers and workloads in the cloud should be seamless, with the organization being able to deploy to any of the three cloud providers based on need, geographic demand, or redundancy.

Integrated and Automatic Security

Security measures that are difficult to apply or difficult to use will not be implemented. Successful DevSecOps emphasizes "secure by default" but also unobtrusive security. Role-based access control is used in a ubiquitous manner. Finding a security problem after go-live is good, assuming that attackers have not yet found it. But finding that security problem after go-live is not optimal. Scanning tools are necessary post-production, but security needs to be shifted left and automatic.

Flagging security issues when code is committed and pushed and then opening tickets with the developer for remediation shifts the responsibility for security to the left side of the development pipeline. An easy example is storage of credentials or secrets within code or configuration that is potentially visible to those who should not see those secrets.

Instead of even getting to the point of needing to store secrets, the type of information stored as secrets should be made available to the developer through the tooling itself. Kubernetes handles secrets in a way that enables an administrator to configure access to view and use the secrets, for example.

Linux Everywhere

Whether serverful or serverless, Linux is the backend driver for DevSecOps. From a practical standpoint, that means promoting tools that are either Linux-based or work seamlessly with Linux. An example of an antipattern is monitoring software that requires an agent to run on the host. The agent itself is a security vulnerability. Rather, we favor software that utilizes least privilege and integrated tools like SSH to gather information. Linux-related skills, like utilizing the command line and understanding the architecture of Linux, should be promoted within an organization.

Refactor and Redeploy

When there were only a few physical hardware servers running many different services, significant value was placed on optimizing resource usage and troubleshooting problems as needed because deploying another instance was simply not possible without significant delay to acquire new hardware. Today, less emphasis is placed on optimization and troubleshooting in favor of refactoring during the next iteration.

Efficient use of resources is still important, but time spent doing so is often more costly than a ground-up rebuild. Resources like memory and processor are enough of a low-cost commodity that deployment of another instance is also less costly than determining the root cause of the failure. Evidence of this is no further than anyone who has ever had to "turn it off and then back on again" in response to a problem with a computer or device. Make no mistake: rebooting should not be a solution and is an indication that something is wrong within the underlying software or operating system. But rebooting is frequently easier than finding the root cause for one-off problems.

Summary

This chapter shared patterns that are frequently found at organizations as they journey along the DevSecOps path. Organizations striving to add DevSecOps practices sometimes add bits and pieces of technology in hopes that the tech will solve the problem. But culture needs to come first, and then add tech where it makes sense. Tech can always be added, but it can be difficult to extract processes from tech once that tech becomes embedded. Avoid adding technical debt to solve technical debt.

Ports and Protocols

Some common ports and protocols are described in Table A-1. See Internet Assigned Numbers Authority (IANA) (*https://www.iana.org/assignments/service-names-port-numbers/service-names-port-numbers.xhtml*) for the definitive reference. It's worth noting that IANA will frequently assign both the TCP and UDP ports to the same protocol even though the protocol only uses one or the other. DNS is a common exception because it uses both UDP and TCP in regular operations. Unless otherwise noted, I've included the more common protocol (TCP or UDP) here.

Table A-1. Common ports and protocols

Protocol	Port(s)	Description
SMTP	TCP/25, TCP/465, TCP/587	Simple Mail Transfer Protocol used for transferring mail between Mail Transfer Agents (MTAs) such as mail servers. Ports 465 and 587 are SSL-protected (SMTPS) ports.
DNS	UDP/53 and TCP/53	Domain Name System protocol is responsible for hostname to IP and IP to hostname resolution along with providing information for a domain such as its mail exchange (MX) records for email and other information. TCP is typically used for zone transfers between authoritative primary and secondary DNS servers. The */etc/hosts* file overrides DNS resolution on a given machine.
HTTP/HTTPS	TCP/80 and TCP/443	Hypertext Transfer Protocol without SSL uses port 80, while the SSL/TLS version uses port 443.
DHCP	UDP/67 and UDP/68	Dynamic Host Configuration Protocol is used to assign IP address, netmask, and other basic network stack information to clients on the local network.
SSH	TCP/22	Secure Shell is the primary means for administering servers and equipment across the internet. Provides end-to-end encryption.
ICMP	None	Internet Control Message Protocol is typically manifest through the `ping` command, but `traceroute` also sometimes uses ICMP. ICMP is frequently used to determine if a host is alive and responding but can be blocked by a firewall and thus is not always accurate.
ARP	None	Address Resolution Protocol is used to translate MAC (Media Access Control) addresses to IP addresses. Like DNS with an */etc/hosts* file, you may need to fake an ARP entry for testing.

Command Reference

This appendix includes commands that will be helpful for the DevSecOps practitioner. The commands included here are not meant to be an exhaustive list of every command that you will ever need, but rather some commands that might be useful for troubleshooting. Some commands covered in this appendix are built into the shell, while others are dependent on other software being installed.

Basic Command-Line Navigation

For those coming from a graphical world, facing a blinking cursor at the command line can be slightly terrifying. Even knowing how to navigate to get a file list or how to get back to your home directory can be helpful, though. When you're using an interactive shell program like bash or zsh, the prompt itself is usually informative and can be configured from system to system.

The command prompt will typically include some type of indication of the current directory. The tilde character (~) is usually an indication that the current directory is your home directory. You can always find out what directory you're in with the pwd command. You can always get home by typing:

```
cd ~
```

View the manual for these or other commands with the man command. Certain commands, like cd, are built into the shell itself. In these cases, view the manual for the shell. For example, to view the manual for zsh, type:

```
man zsh
```

If you're unsure what shell you're using, there are a few ways to find out. First, the env command should have a line indicating SHELL=. Another way to find out what shell you have is to view the */etc/passwd* file on Linux. Yet another way is by using the chsh command. When you type chsh, you will be shown the current shell. Press Ctrl-c to exit out of the chsh command, otherwise you might change your shell!

If you need to determine what username you're logged in with, type:

```
whoami
```

Directory Listing

Obtain a list of files and directories with the ls command. The ls command has many options that are useful and necessary depending on the situation. The -la option is useful because the options cause the ls command to show all files, including dot files or those that begin with a . in their name. The output also includes file permissions and ownership.

```
ls -la
```

It's also helpful to display files in a certain order at times, like the most recently edited file. For that, I typically execute:

```
ls -latr
```

The -t option sorts by time, and -r sorts in reverse. The combination then displays the most recently edited file at the bottom of the listing, thus saving the need to scroll or use a pager.

Pager

While on the subject of pagers, Microsoft Windows includes the more command, but a better option found on macOS and Linux is the less command. Less is more, except better. Use the less command to stop output from scrolling. With less, you can move backward and forward within the output, search backward and forward, and many other tasks. View the man page for the less command to see all options and their explanation.

Command Recall and Tab Completion

Use the up arrow to recall the last command that you ran. Continue pressing the up arrow to move through the history of commands. Depending on the system, you may only see the commands that you ran during the current session or you may see commands from a previous session as well. The down arrow scrolls forward.

If you find a command that you previously ran but now need to change one single option at the beginning of the line, you could use the left arrow to move character by character backward through the command or use Ctrl-a to move the cursor to the beginning of the command line. Ctrl-e moves the cursor to the end of the line.

As you're typing, use the Tab key to complete commands, files, and folders. Be mindful as you do so because the shell will do its best to disambiguate objects but may not always choose the one that you want.

As it relates to command recall, the `history` command shows a certain number of commands that were previously executed, where that "certain number" is dependent on system and configuration. Some systems are configured to clear history on exit, while others keep history seemingly from the beginning of time.

Creating Directories

The `mkdir` command is used to create directories. Add the `-p` option to create an entire hierarchy of directories at once rather than creating each directory one by one.

Changing Permissions and Ownership

As shown previously, the `ls -la` command and options show ownership and permissions for files and directories. Change permissions with the `chmod` command. You'll see combinations of two ways to change permissions, either octal or symbolic. Which you choose is somewhat a matter of preference.

Regardless, if you see advice to change permissions to 777 (octal) or `ugo+rwx` (symbolic), then you can be reasonably assured something is wrong. That permission set enables user, group, and other the ability to overwrite/delete the file or directory. There is almost always a better solution, noting that sometimes you might change something to 777 for troubleshooting temporarily.

See the manual for `chmod` for information on setuid and setgid bits.

Changing ownership is done with the `chown` command. On most systems, you can set both the user and group at once, as follows:

```
chown suehring.users test.txt
```

That command changes the owner to *suehring* and the group to *users* for a file called *test.txt* in the current directory.

Screen Is Your Friend

A long time ago, a senior network engineer said, "Screen is your friend," and that phrase stuck with me, and now I pass it along to you. The `screen` command and its cousin `tmux` are two commands that can be game changers when they are discovered. Both enable long-running interactive shell sessions to run in the background.

I will leave it to you to further research each command.

Using grep

The grep command helps to locate specific information in output. There are numerous ways to do so, but grep is fairly common when searching files for specific strings. For example, if I want to search for Kubernetes YAML files that use a custom namespace, I could use grep as follows:

```
grep namespace *.yaml
```

That command will search every *.yaml* file in the current directory for the word "namespace." Add the -r option to make the search recursive, into directories below the current:

```
grep -r namespace *.yaml
```

Finally, make the search case-insensitive with the -i option:

```
grep -ri namespace *.yaml
```

Note that you might use the find command to enable a more granular file search.

Using touch

While writing this section, I also used the touch command to create a file. The touch command creates a file, if the file is not already present, or changes the timestamp of the file if the file already exists.

DNS with dig

The dig command can be used to help troubleshoot several different types of DNS issues. This section contains the commands along with expected output. The full output is included in the first example and is truncated for certain other examples where the full output isn't needed. In addition, line numbers have been added to the first example to help identify the line in the narrative explanation.

The output that you receive will vary in several ways. Notably, the version of dig that is returned may be different, but so can answer identifiers, response times, message sizes, IP address, and other ephemeral data.

Determine Address for a Host

This command determines the address for a host.

Command

```
dig.www.example.com
```

Output

```
1  ; <<>> DiG 9.16.37-Debian <<>> www.example.com
2  ;; global options: +cmd
3  ;; Got answer:
```

```
 4  ;; ->>HEADER<<- opcode: QUERY, status: NOERROR, id: 46608
 5  ;; flags: qr rd ra; QUERY: 1, ANSWER: 1, AUTHORITY: 0, ADDITIONAL: 1
 6
 7  ;; OPT PSEUDOSECTION:
 8  ; EDNS: version: 0, flags:; udp: 4096
 9  ;; QUESTION SECTION:
10  ;www.example.com.              IN      A
11
12  ;; ANSWER SECTION:
13  www.example.com.    300     IN      A       93.184.216.34
14
15  ;; Query time: 4 msec
16  ;; SERVER: 172.31.0.2#53(172.31.0.2)
17  ;; WHEN: Mon Jun 05 14:35:04 UTC 2023
18  ;; MSG SIZE  rcvd: 60
```

Explanation

The output from this and other dig commands will include the version number as shown in line 1. Lines 2 and 3 display a summary of the options used or implied on the command line and the header text for the response. Line 4 is the first line of interest for troubleshooting. Specifically, the status field response contains NOERROR, indicating that the query was successful. When the host or domain isn't found, the status field response will be NXDOMAIN. Line 5 contains other useful information, including the various fields, typically two letters each, called flags on line 5.

The flags contain indicators about the query and its response, such as whether the response came from an authoritative nameserver for that domain. In the example output, the flags are qr, rd, and ra. The qr field is used to indicate if this is a query (0) or a response (1). The rd and ra flags indicate recursion desired and recursion available. More information on the header fields can be found in RFC 1035. The commands for determining authoritative nameservers are included later in this appendix.

Lines 6 through 11 are related to Extended DNS (EDNS) and are not relevant to the appendix. Refer to RFC Editor (*https://www.rfc-editor.org/info/rfc6891*) for more information on EDNS.

As you might have gleaned from the output, line 12 begins the answer section. Line 13 contains the hostname that was queried, *www.example.com*, the time-to-live (TTL), the type of record (A for address), and the IP address. If this same query were executed again, the TTL value would be lower because of the time elapsed.

With two important caveats, the TTL being used by this local resolver will reset on the next query after 300 seconds elapses. The first caveat pertains to a change in the TTL. After this TTL expires, another query will be sent to the authoritative nameserver. If the owner of the domain changes the TTL, the next query after the 300 seconds elapses will then obtain the new TTL. The second caveat is related to other queries. If someone else queries this local resolver for the same record, then your results around the TTL may vary accordingly.

As it relates to DevSecOps, the authoritative nameserver controls the TTL. If you control a domain and need to lower the TTL, then you need to ensure ample time so that existing cached responses expire and those other resolvers all over the internet then re-query for the authoritative answer.

Line 16 is the next relevant line within the output of a typical dig command. Line 16 contains the IP of the server that provided the response. There are times when you want to query a particular server, whether a local resolver is providing incorrect answers or whether you want to query the authoritative nameserver.

Changing the Server to Be Queried

dig enables easy server changes through the @ symbol. This section shows the syntax for querying a different nameserver for *www.example.com*.

Command

```
dig www.example.com @8.8.8.8
```

Output

The full output will not be included here, but note that the server changed. This is displayed toward the bottom of the output:

```
SERVER: 8.8.8.8#53(8.8.8.8)
```

Explanation

The @ symbol changes the server to which the query will be sent. It's worth noting that you can @ any server, but servers will typically only respond to queries related to domains for which the server is authoritative. Exceptions are resolvers such as 8.8.8.8 and others.

Finding the Authoritative Nameserver

There are two methods for finding the authoritative nameserver, both of which are helpful for troubleshooting and can find different answers at times. The first command is whois, which queries databases of registered names. A portion of the output from whois contains the nameservers as registered. This is the same data that is then queried by the root servers for DNS. Therefore, if the whois data is incorrect, then queries will not be sent to the correct DNS servers.

Another portion of the output from whois is the expiration for a domain. If the domain wasn't renewed in time, then it may be reported as an outage. This happens more often than you might think and only takes a moment to troubleshoot and solve.

The second method for finding the authoritative nameserver assumes that everything is correct with the registrar through whois. The dig command can be used to query for NS records, that is, nameserver records for a domain.

Command

```
dig example.com ns
```

Output

Within the output, notice that there are two answers, and the ANSWER flag indicates as such:

```
;; flags: qr rd ra; QUERY: 1, ANSWER: 2, AUTHORITY: 0, ADDITIONAL: 1
```

Note also that the flags are the same, and there is no aa flag, indicating that the answer received is not authoritative or did not come from the authoritative nameservers for this domain.

The answer section is as follows:

```
;; ANSWER SECTION:
example.com.            300     IN     NS     a.iana-servers.net.
example.com.            300     IN     NS     b.iana-servers.net.
```

Explanation

Within the answer section, the TTL is familiar from an earlier explanation within this appendix. The record type is NS, indicating that *a.iana-servers.net* and *b.iana-servers.net* are NS records within the *example.com* domain.

But misconfigurations happen, and sometimes the NS records that exist in a domain can be slightly misleading. The method used in this section simply looks for NS records in the domain. A more complete answer can be found by using the +nssearch option or querying for the Start of Authority (SOA) record. Here are examples of both.

Command

```
dig example.com +nssearch
```

Output

```
SOA ns.icann.org. noc.dns.icann.org. 2022091294
    7200 3600 1209600 3600 from server 199.43.133.53 in 47 ms.
SOA ns.icann.org. noc.dns.icann.org. 2022091294
    7200 3600 1209600 3600 from server 199.43.135.53 in 55 ms.
```

Explanation

The output from the +nssearch query displays the SOA record information for a given domain. Notice that the SOA record indicates *ns.icann.org* is the authoritative nameserver for *example.com*. The SOA query type can be used as well.

Command

```
dig example.com soa
```

Output

```
example.com.    3600    IN    SOA    ns.icann.org. noc.dns.icann.org. 2022091294
        7200 3600 1209600 3600
```

Explanation

The output when querying an SOA record type contains the domain serial number along with the various caching time values explained in Chapter 2 and in the DNS-related RFCs.

An additional note about the output in this section and for all dig commands. You can add the +short option to shorten the response output, like this example:

```
dig example.com soa +short
```

Personal preference and the task that you're trying to complete with dig will dictate whether you use +short. From my own personal experience, if I'm using dig to troubleshoot a DNS problem that others couldn't figure out, then I'll typically leave the full output enabled.

Querying the Authoritative Nameserver

Combining the previous two examples, querying a different server and finding the authoritative nameserver is helpful for obtaining an authoritative response. If you are on a troubleshooting path that has taken you here, then you should also plan on querying both (or all) nameservers because there are times when the nameservers provide different answers, usually due to error or misconfiguration. However, as noted in an earlier section, the NS records within *example.com* point to *a.iana-servers.net* and *b.iana-servers.net,* but the SOA record indicates *ns.icann.org.*

Querying *a.iana-servers.net* looks like this, which should look familiar from earlier in the appendix.

Command

```
dig www.example.com @a.iana-servers.net
```

Output

The output contains the status flags related to the query along with other information. Output has been truncated to the lines relevant to this section.

```
;; flags: qr aa rd; QUERY: 1, ANSWER: 1, AUTHORITY: 0, ADDITIONAL: 1
;; WARNING: recursion requested but not available

;; ANSWER SECTION:
www.example.com.        86400    IN    A    93.184.216.34
```

Explanation

First, examine the flags and note that the aa flag is present, indicating that this is an authoritative answer for the query. Notice, too, the new WARNING line that the query asked the *iana-servers.net* server to recurse but the server refused to do so. An answer for the query was provided, though.

Another method to find or verify the authoritative answer requires querying the other host that was found through the SOA record, *ns.icann.org*. The authoritative answer flag `aa` is also present in the response.

Finding Mail Servers

The `dig` command is helpful for troubleshooting email delivery issues. The MX record type contains the mail servers for a given domain. This example uses the *oreilly.com* domain. Best practice is typically to use the *example.com* (or *example.net* or *example.org*) domain, but the MX records are not configured for the example domains, which would cause confusion.

Command

```
dig oreilly.com mx
```

Output

```
;; ANSWER SECTION:
oreilly.com.            300     IN      MX      5 alt1.aspmx.l.google.com.
oreilly.com.            300     IN      MX      5 alt2.aspmx.l.google.com.
oreilly.com.            300     IN      MX      10 aspmx3.googlemail.com.
oreilly.com.            300     IN      MX      1 aspmx.l.google.com.
oreilly.com.            300     IN      MX      10 aspmx2.googlemail.com.
```

Explanation

In this example, the *oreilly.com* domain has five MX records. MX records are unique in that there is the normal TTL, type, and host but also an extra number just prior to the hostname in the response. In the output, that number varies and is 5 for the first two responses, 10 for the third response, 1 for *aspmx.l.google.com*, and 10 for the final host. These numbers represent a cost factor and are configured by the operator of the domain. Lower cost is preferred, and multiple MX records are typically used for redundancy.

If the host *aspmx.l.google.com* is not available, a mail server that has email destined for *someone@oreilly.com* will then try the next highest cost, either *alt1.aspmx.l.google.com* or *alt2.aspmx.l.google.com*. If neither of those hosts are available, one of *aspmx3.googlemail.com* or *aspmx2.googlemail.com* will be tried. Finally, the order of the answers will change from query to query, but the costs associated with each host will only change if the operator of *oreilly.com* changes them.

Finding SPF and TXT Records

The final type of record to be queried is a TXT record. TXT records contain things like Sender Policy Framework (SPF) records, among other things.

Command

```
dig example.com txt
```

Output

```
;; ANSWER SECTION:
example.com.    86400   IN   TXT     "v=spf1 -all"
example.com.    86400   IN   TXT     "wgyf8z8cgvm2qmxpnbnldrcltvk4xqfn"
```

Explanation

In this example output, an SPF record is shown along with another TXT record.

Examining the Root

At its most basic, simply running the `dig` command will display a list of root servers for your resolver:

```
dig

; <<>> DiG 9.10.6 <<>>
;; global options: +cmd
;; Got answer:
;; ->>HEADER<<- opcode: QUERY, status: NOERROR, id: 40011
;; flags: qr rd ra ad; QUERY: 1, ANSWER: 13, AUTHORITY: 0, ADDITIONAL: 27

;; OPT PSEUDOSECTION:
; EDNS: version: 0, flags:; udp: 1232
;; QUESTION SECTION:
;.                            IN     NS

;; ANSWER SECTION:
.                   371846   IN     NS     h.root-servers.net.
.                   371846   IN     NS     f.root-servers.net.
.                   371846   IN     NS     a.root-servers.net.
.                   371846   IN     NS     d.root-servers.net.
.                   371846   IN     NS     i.root-servers.net.
.                   371846   IN     NS     b.root-servers.net.
.                   371846   IN     NS     k.root-servers.net.
.                   371846   IN     NS     l.root-servers.net.
.                   371846   IN     NS     e.root-servers.net.
.                   371846   IN     NS     j.root-servers.net.
.                   371846   IN     NS     c.root-servers.net.
.                   371846   IN     NS     g.root-servers.net.
.                   371846   IN     NS     m.root-servers.net.

;; ADDITIONAL SECTION:
a.root-servers.net.  371846   IN     A      198.41.0.4
b.root-servers.net.  371846   IN     A      199.9.14.201
c.root-servers.net.  371846   IN     A      192.33.4.12
d.root-servers.net.  371846   IN     A      199.7.91.13
e.root-servers.net.  371846   IN     A      192.203.230.10
f.root-servers.net.  371846   IN     A      192.5.5.241
g.root-servers.net.  371846   IN     A      192.112.36.4
h.root-servers.net.  371846   IN     A      198.97.190.53
i.root-servers.net.  371846   IN     A      192.36.148.17
j.root-servers.net.  371846   IN     A      192.58.128.30
k.root-servers.net.  371846   IN     A      193.0.14.129
l.root-servers.net.  371846   IN     A      199.7.83.42
```

```
m.root-servers.net.      371846   IN    A       202.12.27.33
a.root-servers.net.      371846   IN    AAAA    2001:503:ba3e::2:30
b.root-servers.net.      371846   IN    AAAA    2001:500:200::b
c.root-servers.net.      371846   IN    AAAA    2001:500:2::c
d.root-servers.net.      371846   IN    AAAA    2001:500:2d::d
e.root-servers.net.      371846   IN    AAAA    2001:500:a8::e
f.root-servers.net.      371846   IN    AAAA    2001:500:2f::f
g.root-servers.net.      371846   IN    AAAA    2001:500:12::d0d
h.root-servers.net.      371846   IN    AAAA    2001:500:1::53
i.root-servers.net.      371846   IN    AAAA    2001:7fe::53
j.root-servers.net.      371846   IN    AAAA    2001:503:c27::2:30
k.root-servers.net.      371846   IN    AAAA    2001:7fd::1
l.root-servers.net.      371846   IN    AAAA    2001:500:9f::42
m.root-servers.net.      371846   IN    AAAA    2001:dc3::35

;; Query time: 1 msec
;; SERVER: 192.168.1.4#53(192.168.1.4)
;; WHEN: Thu Aug  3 11:29:12 CDT 2023
;; MSG SIZE  rcvd: 823
```

Index

POP3 (Post Office Protocol v3), 47
ports, 161
PowerShell, 19
private keys, Git, 81
processes
    microservices, 13
    reliability, 13
    repeatability, 11-12
    scale, 13
    skills promotion, 10
    speed, 13
    tools, 11
    visibility, 13
protocol layers
    OSI model, 21
    TCP/IP model, 21
protocols, 20, 161
    ARP (Address Resolution Protocol), 161
    DHCP (Dynamic Host Configuration Protocol), 161
    DNS (Domain Name System), 23-24, 161
    FTP (File Transfer Protocol), 31
    FTPS (FTP over SSL), 31
    hostname resolution, 24-27
    HTTP, 29-30, 161
    HTTPS, 161
    ICMP (Internet Control Message Protocol), 22, 161
    IP (Internet Protocol), 21
    IPX/SPX (Internetwork Packet Exchange/Sequenced packet Exchange), 31
    phone conversation analogy, 20
    SCP (Secure Copy Protocol), 31
    SFTP (Secure File Transfer Protocol), 31
    SMTP (Simple Mail Transfer Protocol), 47, 161
    SNMP (Simple Network Management Protocol), 31
    SOA record, 27-28
    SSH (Secure Shell), 31, 161
    TCP (Transmission Control Protocol), 22
    UDP (User Datagram Protocol), 22
public keys, Git, 81

Q

QA (quality assurance), 7

R

RBAC (role-based access control), 44

recalling commands, 164
refactor and redeploy, 159
registries, local (Docker), 108-112
regulatory standards, 60-61
reliability, 13
repeatability, 11-12
repository structure, 98
    per-application, 98
RFCs (Requests for Comments), 23

S

SANS, training, 62
SBOM (Software Bill of Materials), 101
scale, 13
SCM (source code management)
    Git and
        branching, 86-87
        commands, 82
        Gitflow, 87-88
        merging, 87
        setup, 79-82
        tracking files, 83-84
        trunk-based pattern, 89-90
    tools, 60
SCM (source code management), Git and, 79
SCP (Secure Copy Protocol), 31
screen command, 165
scripting, 33
Scrum, 4
SDLC (software development lifecycle), 2-4
    DevOps, 14
Secure Copy Protocol (SCP), 31
Secure File Transfer Protocol (SFTP), 31
Secure Hashing Algorithm–based functions, 52
Secure Shell (see SSH)
security
    as afterthought, 8-9
    automatic, 158
    integrated, 158
security awareness, 61
    free knowledge, 62-63
    log analysis and, 63
    training, formal, 61
security practices, 41
    accountability, 57
        code traceability, 59-61
        site reliability, 57-59
        static analysis, 59-61
    availability, 53

tmux command, 165
tools, 11
top-level domains (TLDs), 24
touch command, 166
training in security awareness, 61
Transmission Control Protocol (TCP), 22
triage, monitoring and, 132
TTL (time-to-live), 28

U

UDP (User Datagram Protocol), 22
unit testing, 90

V

variables, 34-35
visibility, 13
    monitoring, 132

W

while loop, 38
Windows command prompt, 19
wired networks, 47-48
wireless networks, 47-48
WSL (Windows Subsystem for Linux), 19

Z

ZAP (Zed Attack Proxy), 63
    Automated Scan, 71-74
    HUD (Heads Up Display), 68
    installation, 65
    manual scan, 66
        ATTACK Mode, 67
        Safe mode, 67
    targets, creating, 64

About the Author

Dr. Steve Suehring is an associate professor of computing at the University of Wisconsin–Stevens Point, where he teaches courses on a variety of topics, from development to networking to cybersecurity. Prior to joining the faculty, Steve worked in several roles, including as a technical architect, systems engineer, and data security analyst. Steve was an editor for *LinuxWorld Magazine* and has written several technology books.

Colophon

The animal on the cover of *Learning DevSecOps* is a dik-dik (genus *Madoqua*). They are native to eastern Africa and parts of southern Africa and are among the world's smallest antelopes, standing 12 to 16 inches at the shoulder, reaching 20 to 28 inches long, and weighing up to 13 pounds. Their upper bodies range from yellowish gray to reddish brown, while their bellies range from white to tan. Males have ridged horns that grow up to 3 inches long. Dik-diks are named for the alarm calls that females make.

Dik-diks generally live in monogamous pairs and are very shy, spending most of their time hiding in brush. They sleep during most of the day to conserve water, and their long snouts are filled with specially adapted blood vessels that help them shed excess heat as they breathe. Dik-diks have black scent glands below the inside corner of each eye that produce a sticky secretion used to mark their territories.

Dik-diks are considered species of least concern. Many of the animals on O'Reilly covers are endangered; all of them are important to the world.

The cover illustration is by Karen Montgomery, based on an antique black-and-white engraving from *The Pictorial Museum of Animated Nature*. The series design is by Edie Freedman, Ellie Volckhausen, and Karen Montgomery. The cover fonts are Gilroy Semibold and Guardian Sans. The text font is Adobe Minion Pro; the heading font is Adobe Myriad Condensed; and the code font is Dalton Maag's Ubuntu Mono.